PAINTING AND UNDERSTANDING
ABSTRACT ART

PARIS by Leonard Brooks.

PAINTING and UNDERSTANDING ABSTRACT ART

An Approach to
Contemporary
Methods

LEONARD
BROOKS

 REINHOLD PUBLISHING CORPORATION / NEW YORK

ACKNOWLEDGEMENTS

The author wishes to thank the many
contributors to this book—the artists,
the collectors, the museums, the writers whose words
are quoted, those who made invaluable
suggestions; to all these my gratitude, for
without them this book would not have been possible.

To my wife, Reva, whose patience and
photographic skill augmented my efforts, again
my many thanks. Also a bow to readers of my
other books who suggested originally that
I essay this volume.

I am grateful to the authors and publishers who have
granted permission to quote from the following publications:
Abstraction–Creation–Art–Non-Figurative, 1932, No. 1, for
statement of Naum Gabo; Alfred H. Barr, Jr. and
Dorothy C. Miller, (eds.), *The New American Painting—
As shown in Eight European Countries, 1958-1959*, The
Museum of Modern Art, New York, for statement by Philip
Guston; John I. H. Baur, (ed.), *The New Decade: 35 American
Painters and Sculptors*, Published for the Whitney Museum
of American Art by the Macmillan Company, New York, 1955,
for statement by James Brooks; Leonard Bernstein, *The Joy
of Music*, Simon and Schuster, Inc., New York; Sibyl
Moholy-Nagy, (tr.), *Pedagogical Sketchbooks of Paul Klee*,
Frederick A. Praeger, New York; Herbert Read, *A Concise
History of Modern Painting*, Frederick A. Praeger, New York,
Thames and Hudson Ltd., London; Michel Seuphor, *Abstract
Painting*, Harry N. Abrams, Inc., New York; Michel Seuphor,
Dictionary of Abstract Painting, Tudor Publishing Co.,
New York, Methuen & Co. Ltd., London; Francis Henry Taylor,
"The Archaic Smile—the Relation of Art and the Dignity of
Man," *Daedalus, Proceeds of the American Academy of Arts
and Sciences*, Vol. 86, No. 4, Oct., 1957.

Designed by Emilio Squeglio
Type set by Howard O. Bullard
Printed by The Comet Press, Inc.
Color printed by Princeton Polychrome Press
Bound by Publishers Book Bindery

Thus the key to abstract art lies in the discovery of
the self and the exploitation by a suitable technique, of that
hidden store of virgin material which we all carry within us,
and to which we must find a path—and this is perhaps the
hardest aspect of the artist's work—before it can be
brought to light.

—MICHEL SEUPHOR

The message of art is not necessarily a simple message
or an easy one; and it is quite legitimate that a painting or
a statue be meaningless to persons at one level of education
and yet be clear and explicit to those at another level who are
particularly trained to understand it. The same layman who takes
offense at an abstract picture in an exhibition, into which the
artist has put years of self-discipline in logical and orderly
arrangement of abstract or theoretical ideas, will accept without question the right of a university or a research foundation
to publish abstruse mathematical conclusions and equations which
as an untrained person, he can never hope to comprehend.

—FRANCIS HENRY TAYLOR,

Former Director of the
Metropolitan Museum of Art

COLOR ILLUSTRATIONS

CONTENTS

PREFACE

This book is an attempt to put down for the artist, student, amateur painter, and the layman who wants to approach his gallery experiences intelligently, some of the many things—ideas, facts, techniques, and conclusions—that have helped the author in his search for an understanding of what Abstract Art is and means.

One of the difficulties the painter faces when he sets out to write about art is that he is very likely to take too much for granted on the part of his readers. It is easy for him to forget that he himself has passed through many periods of murky misunderstandings as well as inspired, joyous glimpses of the creative process during a lifetime devoted to thinking and working as a full-time painter. The beginner may well be at the start of his aesthetic searching with many basic experiences ahead of him before he can begin to see through the mists to the high points, to a truly deep understanding of art, abstract or otherwise. The painter-teacher may readily forget that only a few years ago he too may have been unreceptive to the many strange new types of painting that were emerging with the changing times and that his growth of understanding had been long and often arduous.

Like most working artists of my generation, I have watched the shifting scene in the art world with keen interest and awareness, admittedly at times with some bewilderment and consternation. When one's apparently steady and well-grounded convictions are attacked and often undermined, one doesn't feel too happy about it. It can become a nuisance and a trouble to have to seek out the foundations of the convictions, to review them and to test their worth. But there is no other choice for the creative person who *must* grow and move with his times. Man's world changes and in so doing new truths, new visions and new vitalities arise which require fresh interpretations and expressions.

Most of us, laymen as well as artists, must deal with new ideas that would have been beyond the furthest possibilities of the imagination only a few years ago. If someone had told me when I was a boy that during my lifetime a man would be whirling in space at more than 17,000 miles an hour and circling the world twenty-two times in thirty-four hours, I would have suspected his sanity. Yet this is happening as I write, and such things will be commonplace, or at least routine, before long when man reaches for and gets to the moon.

In the arts, which reflect and interpret our feelings, reassessments and changes are taking place constantly. The artist who is aware incorporates in his dreams the miracles of man and his relationship to them. Some of the wonderment and mystery of existence must of necessity appear in any good painter's work. Sarah Newmeyer put it well when she wrote ". . . the modern artist looks at both the inner world of mind or emotion and the outer world of the senses as though he were the very first person not only to see but to set forth that world in an art form." His personal statement is put down as a meaningful expression for the artist by a conscious effort to use fresh and vivid images drawn from deep within his own world. Some of these expressions of individual imagery are often puzzling and difficult for those of us accustomed to thinking only in realistic and imitative traditional image-forms. We are unable to enjoy, along with the artist, the feelings and visions he has conjured up for us. Sometimes this is the result of a lack of understanding on our part of what the artist is trying to say. Contemporary art is a vastly varied and complex world. There are many things to say and many ways of saying them; to react to and enjoy this world of visual sensation, we must have a key to the languages spoken to us.

Sometimes we acquire a background for understanding without knowing it. It is there for us, if we will meet the painter halfway and keep our minds open while we make our judgments. Leonard Bernstein in his *The Joy of Music* says:

You're absorbing new art all the time, much more than you may consciously realize. . . . The innovations of James Joyce are to be found in some paperback novel you may buy for a quarter in the drugstore. Or when you are looking at a chewing-gum advertisement on the bus, you may be admiring some version of Mondrian or Miró. And while you're watching a play on television, the background music may be by Bartók.

The many changes and countless theories that have grown up about the Abstract Art movement during the last sixty years have been discussed and fought for, derided and praised, accepted and rejected in countless articles, books and verbal fireworks. Much of this is valuable as a clarification process, as a record of styles and as a search for expressive means to produce a valid art for our times. The mountains of art books offer exquisite color plates and reproductions for our delight. Histories of art and courses in art appreciation are more popular today than ever. Unfortunately, few of these have much value when, as students of painting, we approach the palette and brush and face the canvas. The brilliant phrases of the professional art critic and aesthetician are of little help at that moment. A few words from a practising painter and experienced teacher will lead more directly, more straightforwardly, through the tortuous paths of creative painting.

"Painter's talk" is compounded differently than the learned evaluations and essays of the art critic and art scholar. This is the only real justification for the painter who has the temerity to put down in words his ideas and thoughts about his own work or the work of other painters. His words, at least, are tinctured with turpentine essence, the odor of oil paint clings to his pages, and granting him some writing ability, we may look for advice and help to solve precise painting problems that are of immediate concern to the painting student.

Admittedly, a teaching book about Abstract Art may seem out of place; the freedoms associated with Abstract Art may appear to be incompatible with formulated disciplines of a traditional kind. Nevertheless, there are some facts and criteria that may help in the study of the actual practice of making abstract paintings. These techniques are only extensions of other well-known forms of painting derived from older and more classic ways of working.

This book is not a "defense" of abstract painting. That has been done in the past by the defenders of new kinds of painting who drew upon all their forces—at times to a fanatical degree, dismissing all other ways of working—to push through the revolts needed to topple set and accepted traditions that had grown tired and weary. The chart on page 9 shows some of the historical leaves that grew from the classical roots and foundation tree which sprouted its first shoots many years ago. Most of these cycles of change mark high points of experiment and forward steps that led the painter toward a fuller, freer expression. Though interlocked and many times overlapping in intent and direction, these many schools and "isms" helped to free the painter from the shackles of earlier days when strict imitation of natural phenomena was considered the *only* legitimate and serious goal of the professional painter. Today in most civilized circles, there is no need to break swords over the question of Abstract versus Realism because the value and sincerity of much of the Abstract movement has proven itself to be the extension of a legitimate and valid language of the painter.

The obvious abuses of abstract painting are many. Its outward forms are comparatively simple to emulate when compared with the skills needed in the craft of earlier and more traditional techniques of painting. The freedoms of accidental effects, the insistence by many Abstractionists that their private and inner worlds are sacrosanct no matter how unintelligible or non-communicative they may seem to others not familiar with their mystic symbols and private languages—these freedoms allow the charlatan leeway to exploit and imitate the outward appearance of abstraction. Another weakness is the zealous overpromotion, by dealers, of the new and startling at the expense of the quieter and often more profound statement. Who can compete for attention with a twenty-foot canvas painted in blazing vermilion?

In spite of these things, when we look back over the comparatively short time since the first abstract canvases shocked the world, we cannot help but see evidences of the immutable law that says that we get the art that we deserve and for which we are ready. Abstract Art has come into being as a necessary expression of the feelings and thoughts of our age; it has added new dimensions to creative painting; it is part of the constant change and vital searching that energizes every true art. In viewing its many facets, we should keep ourselves unprejudiced and remain willing to share the sometimes uncertain adventures of the many styles and contradictory paths in the abstract and semi-abstract field. Some of these are as diverse and as opposite in direction as are the many different ways of representational painting.

Abstract Art is of and for these times. In its finest form, it is an honest creative search for new and vigorous expressive means. It carries with it all the dangers and abuses of freedom as well as its benefits. Whether it is meaningful and rewarding and whether its teachings will help you as an artist to reach fuller expression of your own creative powers is something only you can decide.

San Miguel de Allende, Gto.
Mexico

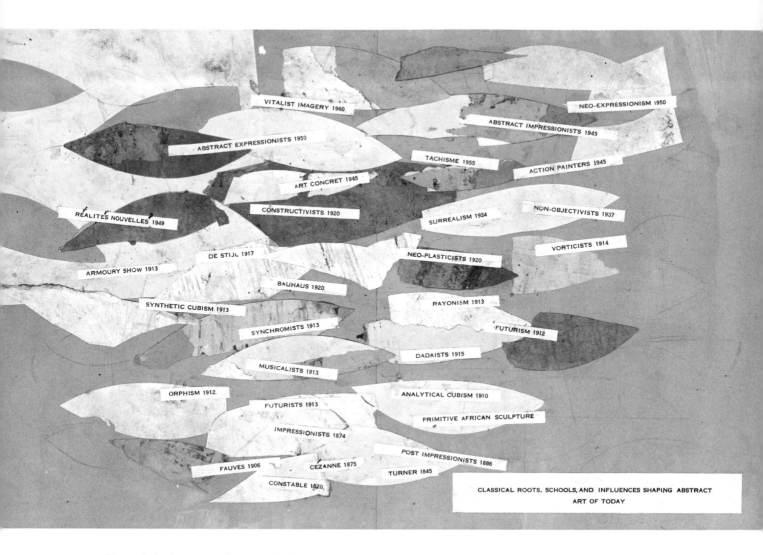

VITALIST IMAGERY 1960

NEO-EXPRESSIONISM 1950

ABSTRACT IMPRESSIONISTS 1945

ABSTRACT EXPRESSIONISTS 1950

TACHISME 1955

ACTION PAINTERS 1945

ART CONCRET 1945

CONSTRUCTIVISTS 1920

SURREALISM 1924

NON-OBJECTIVISTS 1937

RÉALITÉS NOUVELLES 1949

VORTICISTS 1914

DE STIJL 1917

NEO-PLASTICISTS 1920

ARMOURY SHOW 1913

BAUHAUS 1920

RAYONISM 1913

SYNTHETIC CUBISM 1913

SYNCHROMISTS 1913

FUTURISM 1912

DADAISTS 1915

MUSICALISTS 1913

ORPHISM 1912

ANALYTICAL CUBISM 1910

FUTURISTS 1913

PRIMITIVE AFRICAN SCULPTURE

IMPRESSIONISTS 1874

POST IMPRESSIONISTS 1886

FAUVES 1906

CEZANNE 1875

TURNER 1845

CONSTABLE 1820

CLASSICAL ROOTS, SCHOOLS, AND INFLUENCES SHAPING ABSTRACT ART OF TODAY

Some of the leaves on the tree of Abstract Art are shown on the chart above. Named are a few of the major growths and cycles in the development of abstract painting. These changes and styles fluctuate, their influences sweep back and forth in popularity. Some are disdained or forgotten but many are accepted as foundations on which all contemporary work is built.

New forms, new combinations, new discernments are added each year. And between the births and deaths of new isms, a steady flow of genuine painting goes on. Whether it is Abstract, Semi-Abstract, Figurative or Non-Objective, vital and living art seeks its expressive means from all that has ever been produced in the world of art, for the history of art proves that new, odd and perhaps disturbing ways may be considered traditional in a relatively short time. Understandably, however, today's manifestations of new searchings in art are often puzzling and even upsetting to the uninitiated.

"Pop Art," the very latest style of non-art, rejects the emotional "personality projection" of the Abstract Expressionist manner. It is not named on the chart because its position as a genuine art movement is uncertain. Nevertheless, it must be recognized as an opposition of a nihilistic kind that in its way was inevitable. Pop Art is a reflection of the disbelief and cynicism of a younger generation; it has sprung to a prominence that may be only momentary in a historical sense but just the same it is part of the genuine flow of changing values in a difficult world. Where it will lead and what its final value will be can only be decided in the course of time. The true artist considers all methods, past and contemporary, in his effort to find a language expressive of his times.

INTRODUCTION

What is "Abstract" Art?

Trying to define the precise terminology of "abstract" in its purest sense could result in a discussion that could easily fill this book. If you consult American authorities, you will find that geometric abstraction has a somewhat different connotation from what it means in Europe. Abstract, Non-Figurative, Non-Objective, Semi-Abstract, pure Abstraction, Non-Representational—where does one begin and the other end?

Picasso considers that there is no such thing as "abstract" painting; he feels that *all* art is seen in terms of its abstract qualities whether it is in the figurative idiom or not. In the *Dictionary of Abstract Painting* (Seuphor) the definition of Abstract Art is ". . . all art that does not recall or evoke reality regardless of whether that reality be the point from which the artist started or not." True abstract painting, it explains, should avoid representation, even of an accidental kind, or the depicting of any subject whatsoever. Its color, form, and textures exist for themselves alone depending on no reference to any external reality.

This definition would exclude such paintings as those of the Cubists wherein the designs are derived from subject matter and natural forms that have been "abstracted"—that is to say *transposed* from the subject and containing many hints of what the original natural form was. Even the most extreme Cubist distortion has some elements of the face, figure or guitar and wineglass still evident, and therefore would give us a "Semi-Abstraction." Under this definition of Semi-Abstraction, used in Seuphor's *Dictionary of Abstract Painting,* you will look in vain for the inclusion of Picasso or Braque in the listing and illustrations. They will be found, along with many other painters who are not pure Abstractionists, in

Dictionary of Modern Painting.

The term "Non-Figurative" seems to please many artists who are in search of a word to describe a painting without figuration or representation of visual objects and forms. This term is used to describe most painting that depends on abstract and plastic qualities alone for expression and meaning. "Non-Objective," a term losing its force of late, was popular some years ago when the Guggenheim Museum in New York opened its doors. It describes a "pure Abstraction" of the kind created by Kandinsky in which the image is regarded as being rejected. And yet those circles and forms? Can we help equating a flat yellow circle with the sun or moon?

For our purposes in this book, we will keep to the simplest of definitions without worrying too much about an all-embracing and exact meaning of "abstraction." In its larger sense, abstraction can include pictures in which the transposing of the natural scene to a plastic form far removed from reality has been the chief *modus operandi* in the mind of the artist. Because of the many relative stopping places on the road to final "non-figuration" or the purest of abstractions, this large and very broad banner of abstraction will include many artists who, purists may argue, are really listed under the wrong flag.

Such a definition will allow us to survey some of the main currents of abstraction in the last half-century and the experiments of a number of artists whose work was to lead to the many styles of pure abstraction found in contemporary art today. Along with a brief background of this history, we will examine a number of the painting problems and technical problems involved in the search for new and fresh ways of expressive semi- and non-figurative painting.

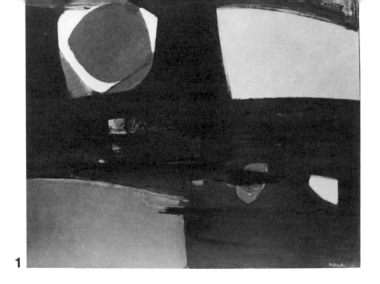

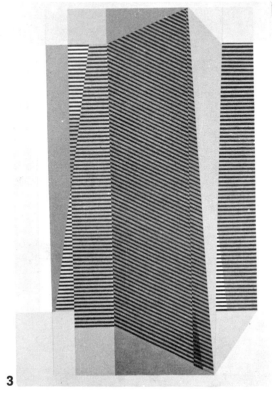

1

4

2

3

5

6

The Dilemma of Choice

As a painter, whatever understanding you have at the moment or may acquire as you work and study further, the question will constantly arise—"What is *my* way of painting; what *really* interests me; what is the natural direction for *my* work to go?"

Beginner, experienced artist, or student, there seems little point in taking up the brush until some pre-assessing of the qualities one seeks are made lucid and defined, if not sharply, at least into a foundation on which work can grow and evolve into a personal statement.

In the past, with its slower pace and time for contemplation, the artist was able to mature at leisure in a safe world of descriptive naturalism. Nature—landscape, man himself and his world—was circumscribed and was relatively secure compared to the age of anxiety and tension in which most of us live today. The "romantic" age produced its own symbols; the manners and the realistic interpretations of this earlier world cannot serve us today in the same way they served our forefathers. This is not to say that we cannot enjoy and be moved by the creative masterpieces of other times, but it does pose a problem for the man who is to create and work with the expressions and feelings of his time.

Part of the chaos in the painting world today—the lack of standards, what is considered good or bad—comes from throwing away standards that are no longer of much value to us in making judgments about contemporary paintings. We cannot apply the same critical eye to assessing an abstract painting as that applied to scrutinizing a Renaissance canvas, a nineteenth century romantic painting, or even an Impressionist canvas. The aims of each are different, their intent at variance. Non-figurative painting has discarded the story telling and the reliance on subject matter. Instead, there is the mystery of the painting itself, evoking an emotional response from the onlooker—space, color, texture, and irradiation of the flat surface of the canvas demanding their own conclusions; organic growth springing from the first stroke on the painting to the last final touch.

Naturally, this "dismissal of the image"—and we will be concerned with this subject further on in the book—is a relative thing. All these marks and colors and textures on the painting, no matter how abstract, spring from *somewhere*. Just how, why, where, and when is a question beyond the scope of this book. The decision to work abstractly is an individual choice only to be decided by the person in whom the inspiration must arise. It is enough to say here that at this point we strike that mysterious wall separating the practical, rational world of everyday from the spirit and *raison d'être* of the arts.

For most artists and students today, the dilemma of choosing a way of working is not the most important problem, but it is often a concern that must be solved before important work can be done. There are so many ways of approaching the canvas, so many attitudes, schools, styles, and isms. Seuphor puts it clearly, "It is a long and complicated task for any young painter to find his personal voice and keep it intact and natural. It is a painful triumph over the self, and when it is carried out sincerely and profoundly, in depth, it is bound to be an heroic undertaking."

How much *more* difficult it is for the amateur painter, unable to give himself the necessary time for the trial and error study needed to find his particular way. Yet, if there is not to be too much wasting of time and fumbling in the dark, the choice *has* to be made, a conscious direction chosen and a sincere conviction felt of where one's goal is to be. And how difficult it is, too, for the intelligent layman who loves paintings to find time to study and understand the complex world of art today.

If you are a primitive—and this is becoming more and more unlikely these days—you need not choose; you merely move in a world of ignorance unaware of all that has happened in the world of art in the past and all that is happening at the moment. The limitations of your mentality will allow you to produce work that has a childish charm of its own, but in the great world of art, unless you are a Rousseau, it will have about as much importance as a child's scrawl.

Another way we can solve the problem of choice is by rejecting all that seems new, turning our backs on the disorder and uncertainty of the complicated art of today and trying to pretend that we are still in another epoch. All is well with the world and let come what may! There is a recipe there awaiting us; the paths are well-trodden and not too difficult to follow. Inured and secure behind a self-created smoke screen, we can go about our task of painting pleasant and acceptable pictures in a mode that has plenty of approval still, whose limits are well-defined, and whose painterly problems have been mostly solved for us.

But if we throw ourselves into the stream of contemporary ways, we must be prepared to withstand the buffetings and uncertainties of the open water. How much easier it is to tuck ourselves safely away in some quiet lagoon much nearer the firm and settled shore!

Whatever we decide to do, or whether we find a compromise for our particular needs and personalities, the questions remain—what kind of painter do we want to be? What are we seeking? Against what standards do we wish to measure ourselves? On the answer depends our stature and our worth as truly creative individuals, no matter at what point we may be at this minute, or from where we may start.

Abstraction by Leonard Brooks

The Cultivated Eye

"Reading" a truly Abstract painting is in a way an art in itself. To react to the sensuous interplay of forms, colors, spatial delineations and plastic qualities of the Non-Figurative painting without thinking of the painting as "a story without words" requires training the eye and mind to a highly receptive degree, if one is to receive the full measure of the work of art. How many patrons of the arts, indulging their love of color and their delight in decorative design and devices, miss the full appreciation and joy of deep perception and are unfulfilled when looking at pictures?

Certainly the art of seeing fully requires the same intelligence demanded of a skilled listener to music—particularly of a contemporary kind—or the reader of a fine novel or poem. Acquiring this skill will probably come much more quickly to one who is intimate with the problems of the paintbox than to the picture-lover who doesn't paint, but this is not always so. I have known painters to become so immured in their own particular viewpoint and problem that they look with jaundiced eye at anything that does not reflect *their own* way of working.

We assume certain understandings on the part of the onlooker as well as on the part of the student painter when visiting an exhibition of old masters or of present day painting. Such knowledges are acquired in many ways—sometimes at school, sometime through self-education, sometimes by a kind of instinctive osmosis that soaks up enough background for the intelligent comprehension of a work of art.

In the highly specialized world of modern painting, some form of tuition is necessary in order to fully enjoy the works of art produced by artists who spend a lifetime exploring and working with their medium. For example, some preparation—perhaps to have studied a Turner—is needed to appreciate the real impact of an Impressionistic picture by Monet or Renoir. We must know that these artists became entranced with painting subjects bathed in light and atmosphere and that their greatest concern was to use pigment in such a way that it depicted man and nature lost in the magic of nature's many changing plays of light and color. What Turner started, Monet and Renoir carried on. Not for them the later concerns of hard lines, clear-cut volumes, structural forms—only

mists, shadows and "lost edges"; light playing on flesh out-of-doors; blue-shadowed days of snow; the changing spotlight of the sun on hayricks at every hour of the day. Without awareness of the artist's intent, we may not only misunderstand but may be moved to derision and scorn as were the dismayed public of Monet's early days. Our uncomprehending eyes and minds will have cheated us, the prejudice of our vision will have triumphed.

When we stand before a "tachist" painting or an early Picasso, further background will be needed. Shorn of the simple putting down of the photographic eye's inventory, bereft of imitation of a subject, size and color and normal proportion twisted and distorted, what have we here? What is the artist putting down for us? What is he after? If we do not have sufficient preparation before we face such work, we are going to be puzzled, unable to perceive what is good or bad about the picture. We will be as lost as the man who picks up the sonnets of Shakespeare, but cannot read.

To develop a cultivated eye, you need not be an artist in the working sense of the word. It will help you if you have painted or drawn pictures, but this is not essential. What you must have done is to have looked at many paintings, thought about them, made comparisons. It helps, too, if you have listened to good music of all kinds, read many fine books, not necessarily about art. It means, in short, to have some kind of standard for judgment. Without this, enjoyment of any art is a doubtful thing and only the most unsophisticated of reactions and appreciation can be yours.

If you are a student painter, the training of your eye is essential both to properly see other painters' efforts, past and present, and to conceive fresh worlds of your own that you will put down on canvas or paper. Knowing what has been done by others will help you to come more quickly to your own conclusions and techniques. For you as a painter, a well-cultivated eye means subjecting yourself to many experiences before works of art, as well as before nature. Such experiences will enable you to expand your visions and so find the influences that will direct your way while you are building a standard for yourself on which you can measure your own efforts.

15

Oil painting by Derek Middleton. A finely worked canvas that uses many repetitions of touch in a carefully considered overall pattern. The abstractions of this English painter working in Paris are beautifully executed within a consciously limited form.

Painting by Roger-François Thépot.

The Image and Imitation

Most artists know that one of the major difficulties encountered by the layman in the understanding of Abstract Art lies in the propensity for relating shapes and colors in pictures to things seen and known. Much of our life is spent in learning to perceive the visual reality of matter, concrete bits of evidence that add up into a material fact—that rough-looking gray scarred surface in an ovoid form is and must be a rock or stone. How cheated we feel when we go over and pick it up to find that we have been fooled and it is only papier maché or plastic, that it is really smooth and weighs nothing. Similarly, we feel a sense of uncertainty, even though we laugh at ourselves while doing so, when we see ourselves reflected in a distorting mirror. We know that we are not really three feet tall and as thin as pictured. It is a relief to see ourselves in a normal glass again, assuring us a safe and normal metamorphosis. But even here, we are not *really* real and are not seen as others see us, for we are of course in reverse.

It is not surprising that when we are confronted with a picturing of forms and shapes on paper or in a painting, we will seek associative images from remembrance of things past, unless we are able to consciously disassociate ourselves from the normal automatic and instinctive reaction.

One of my first experiences in realizing the dangers for the painter in the onlooker's visionary abilities happened many years ago when I sold my first oil painting. I remember it clearly for it was a painting of a snow-clad eminence, strong blue shadows, sunlit ochre-orange rocks woven into what I thought then was a dynamic and well-integrated pattern. My purchaser thought so, too, when he took the picture home, but it was only a day or so later that he was back knocking at my studio door.

Apologetically and rather embarrassed, he stood there with the small canvas under his arm.

"I'm afraid I won't be able to keep the painting," he told me, and continued, "and please don't be insulted if I tell you why. It's the elephant's head! I can't get away from it; every time I look at the picture, it's there."

Now if it had been a rabbit's head, preferably a white one, he continued, he wouldn't have minded so much. But somehow, an elephant's head seemed a bit too much to take in the snowy landscape.

He pointed it out to me and there it was, sure enough—a silhouette formed by the shape of the rock showing through the snow, the accidental shape needing only a suggestive whisper from the mind—"elephant"—to ruin the whole illusion I had been trying to create on the canvas.

Such odd forms pop up constantly in abstract non-figurative paintings and the abstract painter is quick to smudge an edge or destroy the form that is insistently mimetic. If a face or a ship or an animal suddenly appears in the free whirls and markings of an abstract painting, it can be more jolting than if it appeared in a realistic landscape, setting off a whole new series of associations disastrous to the abstract qualities of the painting.

We touch upon this question very lightly for it will quickly be beyond the scope of this book to pursue it further. It is only mentioned to indicate to you how involved the apparently simple matter of painting a picture actually is, once we start to think about it. The confusion about the aesthetics of imitation or mimicry, which is one of the fundamental natural instincts of man as is the urge to draw and paint, never fails to provoke hopeless misunderstandings. If you would like to read more concerning this question you will do well to see the chapter on "Imitation and Creation" in Gilson's *Painting and Reality*. Here you will find a brilliant exposition of why painting is not just an art of imitative technique and how artists have found it useful always to discover, select and bring into sharp focus the elements of reality that please the eye, gradually using the plastic purity of structure alone and dismissing the representational elements that would only confuse the total aesthetic significance.

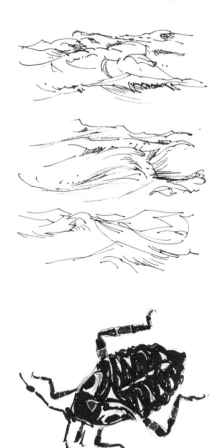

The turn and roll of a vast mid-Atlantic wave; the strange symmetrical patterns on a curious insect; the fortuitous design formed by a casual group of bottles on a shelf, the contours of a man carrying a drum, an old woman shopping, even the curved entanglements of a plate of spaghetti or the vibrating patterns of an unfocussed television screen —all these images provide stimulation for the artist's eye and mind. They are part of the raw material he may call upon when he refashions his own world—his picture.

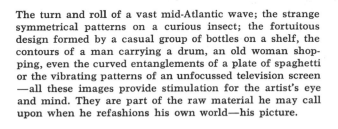

WINTER MEMORY by Leonard Brooks. A blue-and-gray collage. Memories of winter, the melting snow, icy water, pools edge? Gray-green markings and black accents, a walk in the spring woods? Color, subtle and tonal, shape against shape signifying nothing more than itself? Nature reassembled in an oriental mood? Can you react to nonfigurative paintings?

Nature and Abstraction

One of the questions with which, as a painter and teacher, I am constantly confronted is this: "Why does the artist have to run away from nature, from what he actually sees, the reality of what is in front of him?" Why this accent on abstraction and the rejection of the objective world? If it was good enough for the generations of painters down through history, why should many of us in this century be so anxious to dehumanize and dismiss the natural image of things about us?

To answer this in one easy sentence would be impossible; to explain how "reality" is in the first place one thing for the average person's eye and another for the eye of the artist is in itself difficult. You will easily comprehend this when we note that the dictionary defines "reality" as "that which exists independently of ideas concerning it." Most of us have ideas about the things we look at or paint, unless we happen to be an undirected camera. Reality is such a relative thing from the artist's viewpoint certainly, that we must consider carefully before we condemn him for not painting "what is real."

Many aspects of reality that are now accepted as traditional by the most conservative of us were vilified and misunderstood at their inception. We all know how even Ruskin was sued for calling the delicate and misted nocturnes of the Thames River by Whistler "a pot of paint thrown in the public's face." Today, these fragile Victorian night pieces seem very mild and old-fashioned, their blue-gold delicacy romantic and imitative interpretations of actual night. Corot's green and silvery glades, Monet's famed lily-pools, Braque's first still-life paintings, or to go back further in history, Rembrandt's light-bathed subjects—all of these were considered at one time to be the slightly mad visions of artists who should have known better. The *reality* they believed in and created on canvas was not the commonly accepted version; time and the understanding of a more sophisticated eye was needed before these paintings were accepted and loved for their personal and interpretative visions.

With the deserting of common images and the search for a newer and deeper imagery drawn from the inner self, the problem becomes more complex and the projection of this inner consciousness a more abstruse matter. The definitions of "Nature" also expand, and modern man, struck suddenly with a thousand new concepts of what "Nature" is, must expand his vision to include new worlds of seeing and feeling. If he is a city man, as so many of us are, it is very doubtful that he can go on feeling deeply about nature in the form of trees and skies, mountains and streams. These become things he may see on a vacation, or photographed in magazines, but it is much more likely that he

Da Vinci spoke of the fascination to be found in accidental effects of nature, such as stained and worn walls, and how they could suggest compositions to the artist. Here are two examples of nature imitating art. The photograph above is of a blackboard, scored and white-lined, seen in a village station in France; at the right, an ancient, postered wall in Rome is pictured. Such "found art" is often of value to the painter. Similarly, the artists' means—pigments, collages, mixed techniques—may excite the artist. "The materials I am working with frequently supply the shock which suggests my forms, much as the cracks in the wall suggested form to Leonardo," said Miró.

will be moved to put down some reaction to the forms, sounds, noises and feelings of the busy world he moves and lives in most of his days. The chances are that he will have to deal with many mechanical forms and find a way of expressing them unlike that which men found to express the sights, sounds and feelings of early Venetian splendours or the rituals of a deeply religious faith which dominated many generations of painting.

Nature can be many things for many men. Not only the things of the world in front of our eyes, but the world deep within ourselves; not only the imagery of things we know, the objective world, but the world of inventive shapes and forms, for these too are part of ourselves and nature. Sometimes these begin with nature, but often the artist of today denies a direct relationship with natural forms, preferring to dig mysteries out of himself with no previous noting or conscious absorption of the tangible and concrete subject, letting the subconscious direct his brush and hand.

If you would follow through the two sides of thinking—to begin or not begin with nature—you will find a lucid exposition of both sides of the discussion in a beautifully illustrated catalog published by the Whitney Museum of American Art. In it, John I. H. Baur has assembled many examples, in pictures and words, of contemporary artists' thoughts about this problem. This publication, *Nature In Abstraction*, expounding the relation of abstract painting and sculpture to nature in the twentieth century American art world, deserves careful reading by every serious art student.

To the experienced professional artist trained in the traditional skills of draftsmanship and painting techniques, the steps away from figurative subject matter toward Abstract painting are not as difficult or as awkward as we may suspect. The gap between the two ways of working is not the chasm it may appear to the layman, the difference in concept is not a matter of opposite extremes.

This is because the foundations of all fine painting, in any style or mode, have much in common; a bad Abstraction is a bad painting, when analysed in aesthetic terms, for many of the same reasons that a bad figurative painting is considered bad. The cosmic laws of balance, harmony, pictorial dynamics, rhythms and the over-all integration of form underlie both. A jury of successful artists drawn from academic circles will generally agree on a similar selection of abstract paintings if asked to jury a show, even though they may not work in Abstract ways or even if they have a distaste for Abstraction. In the same way, a group of abstract painters judging figurative canvases usually pick the same winners.

There are basics that permeate all painting, though it is difficult to set them up as rules because their qualities are complex and should not be laid down as inflexible recipes for picture-making. We need not prove that Rembrandt would be painting differently if he had lived in the nineteenth century, and even more differently if he lived and worked today. In any age, as a genius and an innovator, he would be aware of the world he lived in; today, Rembrandt would react and paint in the ways of a twentieth-century man, just as in his own day he reacted as a man of his own century.

Today, the artist has available to him the vast storehouse of techniques developed by great artists of the past, and he also commands the new techniques and experimentations of present times. Based on such knowledge, he uses whatever means and creative attitudes he finds necessary for the expression of his feelings about his world. Some traditional means are scrapped; we know how perspective laws have gradually become of questionable value to modern painting. The soft fuzzy edge of the Impressionist has disappeared in favor of clarity, structure and the "hard edge." A new reality shorn of imitative interpretations of the objective world has been explored, in which many artists strive to make concrete the world of the unknown and subjective feelings of themselves and mankind. Like the shifting sands, these new ways of working change their shape and are never fixed and immutable. When Paul Klee said, "We are searching for the essence which lies behind the fortuitous," we have a clue to the attitude of the painter today.

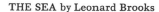

THE SEA by Leonard Brooks

Letting Go

We have heard much in these past few years about "action painting" and automatic gestures that can release the timid and inhibited painter from a too conscious and picayune effort when at work. Later, we will penetrate further into the mysteries of such a technique. Even though we may discount this technique as a remedy or enlivening agent for *all* weak-kneed painting and untalented work, we do find that freeing oneself from a too conscious control can bring forth unexpected qualities that have legitimate claim to aesthetic worth. It is a well-known fact that relaxation is one of the first things a good violin player is taught. A tight nervously clenched hand and stiff wrist—all beginners have it—cannot produce the limpid and flowing tones of relaxed control.

Perhaps we can digress here for a moment and tell a little story—one which, until this moment, I have kept hidden away in my secret archives of memory, for it is a story that still makes me feel foolish, if not a bit ashamed of myself.

It was during war-time and I was somewhere in Canada on the seacoast, dispirited in spite of a week's leave from the Navy. Painting, it seemed, had been forgotten; the pleasant hours of sketching and drawing were peacetime dreams. I felt in a bitter mood—the large picture I had painted a year before had been submitted to the National Gallery and had been rejected.

It was in this frame of mind that I finally visited a friend and watched him at work in his studio, painting, of all things, a rather innocuous picture of a pot of yellow daffodils. Sensing my depression, he kindly offered me the use of his watercolor table, some paints and a fine large sheet of *Arches* paper.

"Why don't you just relax and enjoy yourself?" he said.

"Relax?" I answered. "With the world going mad. the days filled with killing and disaster?" What good were the efforts of man, especially painters and poets? What significance the gentle arts now? Even the world of painting was infected with disillusion and despair including (I thought to myself) the juries of exhibitions who refused perfectly good paintings and accepted only those wild Abstract sensations that seemed to be taking over all art shows.

In this spirit, I took advantage of my friend's offer and reached for his brushes.

"I'll show you what they want," I said, "and how easy it is to do."

I was angry and so was my brush, angry enough to forget the usual habits of former years of painting, yet relaxed in a consciously nervous manner. Let the brush fly where it wanted, destroy that smug white magnificent 300 pound paper! No careful drawing, no worrying about the composition, no decisions about space. I was ready to outdo the daub-and-splatter technique.

Perhaps this is what they want! Bang went the sponge filled with water. Vitality, no doubt? Splash went the yellow area in the centre of the running wash. Expressionism, did you say? Splosh went the dab of red, the stroke of blue. Drawing? No fuss with that—and into the wet paper quickly I scrawled the jagged forms of waves and the broken lines suggestive of a flotilla of ships in a sombre sea of dirty umber. Rapidly I filled the large sheet, digging out of myself some of the color and the forms of the dark and dirty port of Halifax where I was stationed. No time for tricks or clever techniques, only the heated putting down of elements that seemed to spring onto the paper from deep inside me almost of their own volition. Less than twenty minutes had elapsed.

22

"There," I said, "perhaps that will do it." A few scratches here and there with a razor blade, a soaking up of a too definite edge, and the picture was complete. It was an angry picture, not at all pleasant, a bit messy, but somehow alive. I left it in my friend's studio and it was not until some months later, when I was overseas, that I heard from him. Could he, he wrote, send the picture off to a watercolor show? He had matted and framed it and it looked good. It had been commented upon favorably.

I wrote back and said that he could send it, but not to sign my name. Invent one—Zick or Zock or anything he wished.

Six months later, I was standing in the watercolor gallery of the National Gallery. In it was a selected group of forty watercolors picked from a large international show for a year's travelling exhibition. In front of me stood the man who was to approve my appointment as Official War Artist to the Royal Canadian Navy. Behind me was a strong and effective watercolor of Halifax harbor. It was listed as "Wartime Mood" and was signed by someone named Zick. It took maneuvering but I was able to edge myself and the curator into another part of the gallery.

I tell this story here, even though it is on myself, to underline how so much creative effort is of this nature, springing up within ourselves often from we know not where, often hidden at some source that we have left untapped, or have kept in bondage, chained and inhibited.

In the case of the angry watercolor, looking back these twenty years, I can see now how it was a step forward for me. What began in derision and anger released something of myself that my work had always needed—more freedom, less self-conscious cleverness, a more spontaneous use of my own personal resources and feelings, a relaxed brush but a controlled one.

Perhaps when you find yourself bogging down in a frustrating series of painting sessions, or when the pressures of trying too hard seem to limit your study efforts, an energetic period of just "letting go" may help bring your spirits and your paintings to life.

ROCKY SHORE by Leonard Brooks. Watercolor.

TWO STUDIOS—TWO VIEWS

This is the story of two studios. It will illustrate the point I want to impress upon you—that art, being in essence an expression of the feelings and mores of the times, is ever changing.

For many people painting provides relaxation, a chance to venture into the world of expression in a plastic sense, a chance to use line and form and color, to invent a "little world of their own." For some, this activity means enjoyment, an opportunity to use leisure time in a constructive if not very serious manner. For others, painting becomes a way of life and a dedication. It fills most of their waking hours and the ordinary matters of normal living are fitted into a scheme of existence that permits the painter to pursue a full professional life. For them "art" is a very serious matter and come what may they are ready to form their daily pattern of living around the job of producing paintings.

This dedicated life of the full-time worker in the arts is not such a rare thing as it was even a few years ago. More painters are wielding a brush as a full time job than ever before. Millions more are painting as a secondary occupation. Talent need no longer starve in a garret, and seldom does a good picture—Abstract, Realistic, or in any style whatsoever—go begging.

It was fascinating to me recently to have the privilege of seeing two artists' households where the patterns of existence were determined completely and irrevocably by the painter's creed. Both artists were "Abstract" artists. Here is a short sketch of their studios to illustrate how diverse the world of the Abstract painter can be today—as odd, profoundly contradictory and yet as vitally alive as this contemporary world of ours which it reflects.

Studio One

Pierre is a Belgian painter who lives and paints in a studio on the outskirts of Paris. I met him at an artists' gathering where he was introduced to me as one of the younger Abstract painters who had begun to make their mark in the international art world. He had already had a number of successful Paris shows and had recently sold a large canvas to the Belgian National Gallery.

Studio space is scarce and expensive in Paris, therefore I was very happy to learn that his studio-and-living quarters would be available for four months. Perhaps, he said, I would like to visit him and see it; I might like to sublet it for my intended stay in Paris.

So the next day, my wife and I spent the afternoon with Pierre and his diminutive French wife in their studio-apartment, sipping Calvados while we discussed art and considered the possibilities of taking over the place.

However, before we arrived at this point, we had had a few shocks. The first shock was the location of the studio. The unsavory neighborhood was in a run-down section of Paris near Vincenne Park. The building was a dingy tenement-like structure. And we had to climb up four flights of stairs only to find ourselves in a messy, malodorous hallway. Off this hallway was Pierre's studio. When Pierre opened the door and we stepped into the tiny room that served as combined studio and living quarters, we really had a shock. Both of us paused in amazement, trying not to look too startled or curious, for what we had walked into was not a room—but a picture!

Conceive, if you can, a twenty-by-nine-foot painting by Mondrian suddenly alive in three dimensions—one wall a brilliant orange, the two side walls stark white, the far wall a square of solid black. Against this in neat squares and oblongs, place the scarlet lozenge of a folding bed serving as the only couch in the room; place thin white strips for shelves, suspended from the ceiling by nylon wires and holding a choice number of gaily-jacketed books. Add a few sparse pieces of decorative bric-a-brac, the interior workings of a dismantled piano with wired keys twisted into staccato patterns on a length of moulding hung vertically, as a piece of sculpture—and strangely effective too. A bowl of pears resting on a wheeled glass coffee table and two Saarinen chairs with sheep-skin seats. That was about it.

A pantry pass-through pierced one wall, creating a two-foot opening that led into a closet equipped with sink, burner and shower. This glorified cubbyhole served as a kitchen. A rectangular table, supported by a hinged, flat leg, was attached to the base of the aperture. Pierre proudly demonstrated how the table could be lifted and hooked against the wall in such a way as to close off the opening completely. When this was done, the reverse side of the table became a painting in relief, a circle and three lines in black and white, the collapsible leg forming part of the design.

Against the black wall was an easel; the purest, whitest, most unsmeared easel I have ever seen. Beside it was a high white box on wheels. In this, under a lid, lay the materials for Pierre's painting —all the tubes and cans, brushes and emulsions, rulers and compasses, tacks and hammers. The floor was polished black linoleum.

There was a sparsity about the room that pleased the eye. Everything was placed so *right*, each proportion and division of space lay contentedly under the soft concealed overhead lighting. The room was, in a curious way, a work of art, even if one felt that the composition would fall to pieces if a chair became misplaced or a book or two fell from the slim hanging shelves.

Neat, controlled, formalized, practical; these words came to mind as we studied what was perhaps to be our new home for a time. Both of us, I knew, were secretly wondering how I would manage to paint pictures in such an orderly

atmosphere and how difficult it would be to hang some brown paper over the bright walls without hurting the smooth, unmarked, colored surfaces.

Pierre went across the hall to a closet where he stored his pictures. How much his paintings resembled the studio! How neatly they had been stored away in their cellophane jackets to protect the smooth satin-finished surfaces of the large and small mounted panels which he set on the easel, one after another, for us to see.

Pierre is a "Constructivist" painter and his paintings are cleanly conceived in geometric lines and planes barren of any evidences of spontaneity or accidental qualities. With exquisite taste and selection and the precision of a watchmaker, black lines are incised on the whitest of white backgrounds. Occasionally, a colored line or plane is used, again with controlled simplicity and preconceived design. Nowhere does a brushstroke obtrude itself or a line take off freed from rigid gradation and precise drawing.

Perhaps you can imagine one of Pierre's pictures hung against the wall of his studio. Any other kind of picture would have seemed out of place and slightly ridiculous. A landscape hanging on that black wall would knock a hole in it with the force of a small bomb.

We learned more about Pierre and his work; how he was part of a group of painters who worked in similar fashion and how they all exhibited in one gallery where only Constructivist paintings were shown. We saw, too, plans Pierre had designed for architects–façades for modern apartment buildings, murals and walls broken into geometric lines and colors like his paintings. These were fascinating even though, we thought to ourselves, they would be a bit monotonous if too many were seen at one time.

Perhaps you would not react favorably to the apparently "mechanical" quality of the paintings Pierre and his friends produce. To many of us, such disciplines and limited means seem cold and uncommunicative. Granting that they reflect our contemporary life, most of us still prefer to see such designs used to a functional end, as a decorative style for modern furniture, for carpets or store fronts, not as canvases to hang on our walls for everyday living.

Perhaps, once upon a time, Pierre felt this way himself. On a visit to his home in Belgium, I was able to see some of his earlier work which showed the formative influences that led to his present style of painting. There were large realistic portraits, well-painted and drawn, and a number of early landscapes of the Expressionist kind favored by Permeke, dark and sombre in color. A similar evolution of style can be seen in the work of

Mondrian, who began with typical bucolic landscapes of the Dutch cow-and-pasture type and ended, after many changes and fluctuating directions, with his well-known Neo-Plastic solutions which are nothing more than canvas space divided by colored lines, rectangles and squares. He never used green in his later work.

Note: We did move into Pierre's studio and I did paint in it, but it was not easy. People who are unaccustomed to living and painting in the same small room and putting things back in the exact spot *every time* they use them can get into an awful mess. We did.

Studio Two

Yvonne and Charles are painters who have their studio and house far out in the suburbs of Paris. We left early to visit them in order to avoid the heavy traffic that pours daily over the Austerlitz bridge.

Our visit was pleasant as well as informative. Both painters are warm, outgoing hosts, and we found other painters gathered there that Sunday afternoon to discuss art, exchange criticisms and make plans for future exhibitions. Their large,

rambling old house set in a tangled garden behind stone walls is truly an artist's hideout. When the two painters first moved away from the city, as their canvases grew larger and larger, they rigged up a high-ceilinged workshop in the garage attached to the house. It was not long before their work demanded more and more room. Soon the six huge old-fashioned rooms in the house were taken over, leaving only a small ante-room with a fireplace free of easels and paint pots.

Yvonne and Charles are what we used to think of as Bohemians, if that term means "unconventional" and doing and saying unexpected things. Both are serious, dedicated painters and highly successful ones. Lately, Yvonne has been selling her work to collectors who know what is going on in the international art world, and quite recently she won high honors at the Venice Biennial Exhibition with an immense and lively canvas crackling with the tremendous energy that marks her work. Yvonne has a unique way of working; the tools of her studio are especially geared to the intensity of her execution. Her working palette, running against the long wall of the garage studio, is a most colorful and startling one. It is a ten-foot-long table covered with two-foot wide piles of brilliant colors, pounds of them, which she mixes herself. Broad wooden and metal spatulas—often two feet wide and more—are used to scoop up the mixed paint and transfer it in one wide stroke to the immense surface of the waiting canvas standing on the floor, or what we assumed to be the floor, for every bit of the room is covered with inches of hard dried paint from previous painting sessions.

We should have been warned to wear our old clothes, as we had to be careful not to sit on any of the chairs or lean against anything in the studio —paint was everywhere. However, we were content to stand and enjoy the stack of paintings that Yvonne man-handled and hoisted to the far wall for us to contemplate.

Words are rather useless in trying to describe the paintings. We could list the rich arabesques of mottled rubys and violets, the dancing scarlets and vibrant greens and browns, or describe the thick juicy texture of impastos richly integrated against each other, but the effort is futile; it would be much better to keep an eye open for Yvonne's paintings when you see the next travelling show.

Charles' studio takes up several rooms

downstairs. The main room was once the front parlour of a proud French "bourgeois." Now this room is splashed from floor to ceiling with paint. Paint hangs in festoons from the light fixtures, covers the telephone with several inches of pigment, drips and splatters across the window-panes and walls when flying paint exceeds the bounds of the canvas. Here is "action painting" indeed and evidences of battles with paint mark every inch of the studio, which looks as though a small bomb had dropped among the open gallon-cans of paint standing on the floor.

Charles has his own implements for the fray. Some of them are reconverted sponge rollers and troughs ordinarily used for house wall painting. One of the most interesting pieces of equipment is made from six 6-inch bristle brushes nailed closely together on a flat stick. This makes the biggest brush in the world, I suspect, a brush that can sweep a mighty swath a yard wide across a canvas in one rugged stroke.

We saw only a few of Charles' smaller efforts in his studio. His really important canvases were stacked against the garage outside and covered with tarpaulins to protect them from the rain. They were fifteen- and eighteen-foot canvases, too large to get into the house. To see them, we found it convenient to get up on the garage roof and look down from a suitable distance in order to take in the whole composition at once, as though we were in a vast art gallery.

In the garden were huge slabs of lumber from buildings and wharves, eroded and worn through years of use. These were interlocked and pegged into abstract shapes, finished in tones of white and blue, making handsome decorative pieces for the green lawn.

Here too, paint was in the air almost everywhere.

We breathed it, sat in it, looked at it, and carried some of it away on our clothes as souvenirs.

We have seen Yvonne and Charles many times since our first visit. It is always the same; they are always affable, enthusiastic, always at work. The paint grows thicker on the telephone and the chairs as well as on their paintings. On our last visit, we found that their brown collie dog had turned bright green and we thought we saw some odd-looking brightly-tinted violet sparrows pecking red crumbs on the studio roof. . .

When you come upon a canvas by Yvonne or her husband in the quiet sanctum of some public gallery in Amsterdam or Buenos Aires, the glowing colors and slabs of dry, thick paint burst across the room like multi-colored butterflies of gigantic size, and the strong contrasts of Charles' paintings attract us with their sense of solidity and freedom of execution. Seen away from the paint shop, singly and uncluttered, the paintings sing out with the joy of vital paint surfaces and the strong personal styles imprinted on the canvases. I have had two of them on my own walls for a year now and know how exhilarating they can be. Both painters have put something of themselves into their work. How could it be otherwise with such dedication and such living for paint?

Two studios—two views. Both workshops belonging to Abstract painters, but how vast the difference in their ways of living and working! The contrast is as great, if not more so, than the many ways in which the figurative or "realistic" painter can work today.

Between these two extremes—the formal and the free, the controlled and the accidental expression—are many shades and degrees of abstraction. A number of them are waiting for us to examine in the pages to come.

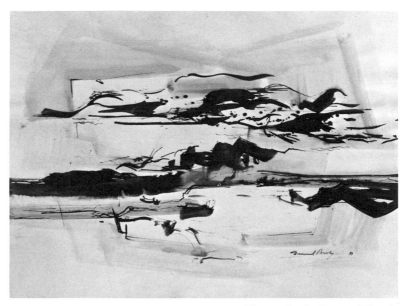

Abstraction by Leonard Brooks

BACKGROUND FOR ABSTRACTION

In reaching toward an understanding of Abstract Art, we are going to look over some of the early theories and directions that painters of many schools formed and used in their search for expressive manners in non-figurative painting. As we intend to do some simple practical exercises in some of the techniques and styles to be studied, the experienced artist-reader who is conversant with these things may want to skip this section and go on to more complicated matters further in the book.

For the student however, these foundation stones on which artists have built contemporary ways of working are indispensable, as they are for the picture-lover and the amateur who wants to understand—and thus enjoy more—the paintings of contemporary artists. These exercises have been kept purposefully simple so that no one need feel he cannot try them for lack of drawing skills. The more advanced student can use more complex figurations but the underlying meaning and point of the demonstration should be kept strictly in mind. In this way, the basic background for understanding such things as "pictorial space" and so forth can be easily mastered before going on to the more complicated theories of abstract picture making.

The Picture Plane and Pictorial Space

"What is all this talk about 'space' in contemporary painting?" This question is often asked by puzzled amateur painters and art students as well as by the viewers who do not paint but are making gallant attempts to comprehend the background of abstract picture-making. Inevitably, they will have come upon "space" in exhibition catalogs; docents in museums will have described with mysterious sweeps of the hand over and "through" the painting before them how the artist has realized "the thrust of the tensions spatially in depth," and how obviously he is a master "who respects the 'integrity' of his picture plane as well as the interaction of the space in which a part is relative to nothing else but that beyond itself in its opposite of volume perception,"—or something equally as confusing and verbose. "Negative space" which refuses to function negatively in the mysterious space that everyone seems to take for granted, "cross tensions and thrust," and other such phrases derived legitimately enough from the painter's pictorial problems are tossed around in a too-often incomprehensible phraseology that even a twentieth-century spaceman would find confusing.

Nevertheless, if we can side-step the effusive verbiage of much art space talk, there are many valuable lessons we can learn and which we must seriously consider about the nature of pictorial space. For even the most skeptical of us, there are valid reasonings and conclusions that have become part of the contemporary artist's heritage from the centuries of research and experiment by artists before him. The scientific explorations of great masters of the past have presented us with many discoveries that form the foundation of our present-day painting concepts. The serious art student will find it fascinating to look over some of these problems of animating the picture surface— the *flat* surface, the flat *space* with *two*-dimensional lines and forms taken from objects in the *three*-dimensional world about us—for in essence this is really the crux of the whole problem.

There is *pictorial* space versus *actual* space and the world of apparent reality that we perceive with our eyes. This difference has been the concern of the artist from primitive times, and in his efforts to record and express his world he has tried many ways and forms to control the illusion of depth on a flat surface.

Since earliest times, man has been intrigued with spatial illusion, from the unscientific thinkings of the first primitive artist down to the sophisticated and complicated geometry of the Constructivists of today. Egyptian, Arabic, Persian,

Middle Ages, Renaissance, Twentieth Century— each age has found solutions to its own times, inventing and using its own conventions of space concepts. Some of these traditions still exist and in the illustrations shown on pages 30 and 31 a few of them will be readily recognized. Why does a Chinese print in the traditional oriental manner still look odd to many of us? What happens to those tables that seem to be standing up in the air, which we see in the Cubist's paintings, the ones where the plate and fruit on it could not possibly rest on the table if what is pictured happened to be "real"?

When the earliest artist we know about, the caveman whose work has been preserved for us on the walls of his ancient home, felt the need to put down a record about his hunting, he was faced with the problem of creating space on a flat or comparatively flat surface of his cave dwelling. How did he show us the illusion of depth? By the simplest means he had at his disposal, the use of the silhouette form set in outline against another silhouetted outline. With this device, he was able to show that one thing was to be conceived as being in front or behind another. The Egyptians did the same thing but went one step further, constructing a ground line on which all figures and objects stood. They also suggested depth by putting the figure in two views at once, the figure being represented with the head in profile while the torso and the rest of the figure was drawn in front view with the two arms flat to the picture-plane. This convention served for many centuries, limited though it may have been.

Elsewhere, the oriental artists of China and Persia were developing their own spatial solutions. The landscape was a major subject of their art and they soon found a way of using the projection of a diagonal line suggestive of recession. On this line, they drew a kind of aerial view, looking *down* on their subject with further objects piling up one behind the other, placed higher on the page as the distance increased. (Thus the use of many long vertical scrolls.) This convention of suggesting space and distance still exists in much oriental art today and gives it some of its charm for those of us trained to see paintings in the occidental perspective convention.

The overlapping of outline and its suggestion of volume can easily be seen in Figure 1. Both the circle and the square provide the suggestion of depth and movement into pictorial space. This overlapping of the forms and the tensions set up between two or more such forms has fascinated many contemporary artists such as Hans Hofmann who uses its spatial movement (push and pull on a flat surface) in much of his work and whose

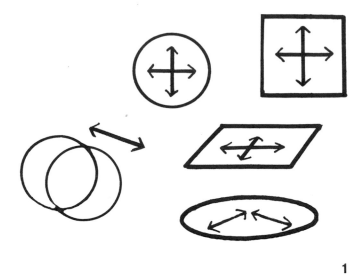

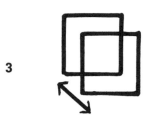

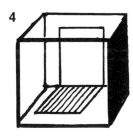

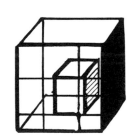

1

2

3

4

1. Space simply defined by the use of circle and square. The flatness (indicated by the crossed arrows) may suggest recession into space when overlappings occur or if the circle or square is tipped.

2—3. The Chinese village drawing makes use of the diagonal moving upwards and through the overlapping houses to provide depth.

4. The cube concept which helped develop the early concepts of space. The grid of lines across the front face of the cube is called the *picture plane.* On it, recession and depth illusion is made and controlled. The right-angle formed by the floor and back of the box was the format on which most oriental "perspective" was drawn.

theories may be studied in the catalog of his 1963 exhibition published by the Museum of Modern Art, New York.

When we turn the square to an oblique angle we have another suggestion of recession. Notice that this is achieved without the use of perspective by using only isometric drawing (equal distance of the parallel receding lines at each end of the figure). This kind of space drawing is the kind the carpenter uses when he wishes to draw a diagram of furniture he will make. It tells the facts of construction without using perspective laws and tells them in a more "realistic" surveying of volume than if I drew it for him the way it *appears* to look to our eyes.

Just how things *seemed* to look was the

fascination that kept scholars and artists experimenting with panes of grid-marked glass and checker boards from the twelfth to the sixteenth century. *Perspectus* (to see through) allowed the artist to draw on an upright transparent surface on which he traced the lines of his subject, using a grid of squares. Thus the first rules of optics for the draftsman and artist were formulated in the early centuries of man's scientific curiosity and many of them remain almost unchanged today.

Figure 6 shows one of the major discoveries. Experiments with the squares on a checker board brought into being the rule of *parallel* perspective —parallel lines receding to a point on the eye-level known as the *vanishing point.* This one-point perspective served the artist for many generations. On this grid, objects could be placed below or above the eye level and infinite space could be suggested by using buildings, roads, and landscape motifs. This discovery was a simple development of the Middle Ages theory of the diagonal (Figure 4) in which the oblique square had diagonal lines at each end leading into space. The cube set on the frontal space of what was known as the "picture plane" allowed the artist to suggest flatness (objects flat and parallel to the picture plane) and recession (objects turned at an angle to the flat picture plane). These recessive forms are easily realized in Figure 5. A grasp of this simple theory is pertinent to understanding the further complications that the artist found in his development of perspective.

Contradictions abounded in the early days of

5. The double diagonal receding into the picture plane was used by the Persians to suggest "going back." The contradiction of the checker-board being an upright pattern (flat to picture-plane surface) was an accepted convention. Patterns and decorations were not drawn in a similar "going back" receding plane.

6. One-point perspective (parallel perspective) was the scientific formula used by the great masters of the early Renaissance. Bruegel, da Vinci and others used its findings for much of their work. "The Last Supper" is a fine example of this formula used to express recession and foreshortening.

7. The medieval artists used an isometric form of perspective without receding parallels. The effect of overlapping was used with many viewpoints seen in isometric form.

8. Two-point perspective. By the fifteenth century, the artist-scientist had solved the problem of projecting the oblique object turned at an angle to the picture plane. Architects and artists quickly became skilled in the use of this new projection, and the two-point perspective theory soon became standard convention for Western artists, until the twentieth century began to question its oligarchy.

A, B, C and D illustrate four tables drawn with the perspective conventions of different epochs. Note the similarity to some Cubist renderings in which the parallel line to vanishing point theory is reversed and the law of "foreshortening" is broken.

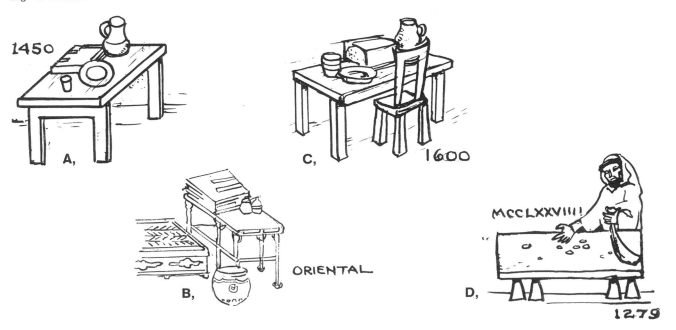

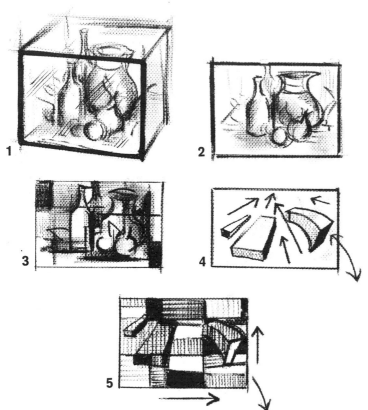

1. The picture plane is defined as the front face of the cube, parallel to the onlooker. On it, flatness or recession can be controlled.

2. Here we have represented the objects on the picture plane with indications of depth and "behindness" by shading and modelling the forms.

3. The flatness of the picture plane has been stressed by using arbitrary horizontal and vertical black accents and lines. There is less feeling that the objects are hanging in the air. They have been tied into the boundaries of the rectangular flat area in pictorial space.

4. Spatial volumes. Movements are set up by using objects representing three-dimensional solids thrusting back into limitless space. We have no idea or indication of the limits of this deep space. Objects float in the air. The eye, seeking relationships, searches for relative distances. An uncomfortable sensation is set up when objects are set in such inconclusive and undefined space.

5. What happens when we impose a flattening grid of horizontal and vertical lines over these objects? New spatial relationships are set up. Now we have depth, interlocking planes on various levels of space, and movements which the eye seeks out and relates to the sides and top of the picture plane. Notice the curved solid on the right. It does not lie flat but comes forward from the picture plane. Such extrusions in a painting can destroy unity. We speak of such areas as "not respecting the picture-plane."

perspective study. Figure 5 shows a common error that was made, an error that gives a decorative charm to many Pre-Renaissance paintings. Depth is depicted with receding diagonals at angles to the picture plane. At the same time, the checker-board pattern is superimposed on this receding floor plane in a horizontal and vertical manner without consideration of the recession of the small squares. Such ways of drawing space were evident in many mediaeval paintings (Figure 7).

A study of Gothic drawings and the paintings of Bosch will provide many illustrations of perspective variants based on theory. Fourteenth-century artists had their troubles in suggesting oblique volumes, but by the fifteenth century the artist-scientists had perfected the science of perspective, with minor exceptions, to a point similar to what we use today, two-point or angular perspective (Figure 8).

With this knowledge from the great age of scientific discovery brilliant renderings were done by master craftsmen who seized upon the new theories to paint a new and exciting visual world never before captured in paintings. The vision of man set the world of art afire with astounding panoramas depicting a thousand architectural wonders, views, and visions both seen and imagined. Bruegel, Veronese, Bellini—the names are many—have their masterpieces in the great galleries for us to see, study and marvel at. No

wonder Uccello used to mutter in his sleep, "Oh, how delightful a thing is this perspective!" (Vasari)

This break-through in capturing the illusive optical illusion of space, set the pattern for many centuries. "Good" drawing became essentially perspective drawing and woe to the student in the drawing academies of Rome or Paris who did not know how to set up or construe the elaborate mathematical equations of perspective geometry and rendering. For four hundred years, the mark of geometrical perspective dominated the seeing of the creative and civilized artist. Only the savage in far lands continued to make his unscientific plastic expressions which were considered naive, strange and not of too much value to a civilized eye. Not until the nineteenth century did the Impressionists and Post-Impressionists such as van Gogh, Gauguin, Redon, Vuillard and others rediscover the value of primitive interpretation as a creative force.

And it was not until the end of the nineteenth century that the artist began to consciously reject the perspective theory as an infallible law essential to his work. Only then, about 1890, did the first signs of rebellion and junking of the supposedly implacable laws take place. Let us consider this rebellion carefully, for its small beginning started the breakaway from the hide-bound perspective tradition to a new and startling art which was to develop into what we know now as the art of the twentieth century.

Modern Concepts of Pictorial Space

1. Cézanne-like drawing from nature to express volume and space related to the picture plane. The emphasis on unity integrated *behind* the picture plane with lines and forms *on* the flat picture plane ushered in a new concept of orderly pictorial dynamics for this century.

2. Van Gogh, influenced by oriental prints, used the diagonal and space motifs of Japanese character in much of his work. Inset is a sketch copied from his painting "Falling Leaves at Arles" which shows the contrast between flatness of tree forms close to the picture plane, and recession of the street set diagonally behind them.

3. An early Cubist style that was called analytical. In 1908, Picasso and Braque made researches into the break-up of volume and pictorial space based on the work of Cézanne. Figures and objects were dissolved, new planar relations were created, still keeping figurative connotations of the objects depicted.

4. A later Cubist style evolved less severely geometric structure. Braque continued this manner of the "fractured image" into his last year—1962. Cubism's influence on twentieth century architecture and design is beyond assessing.

5. Non-figurative painting uses the pure forms of pictorial space without reference to the objective world. The many forms pure Abstract Art may take are infinite and some of them will be studied in the pages of this book.

33

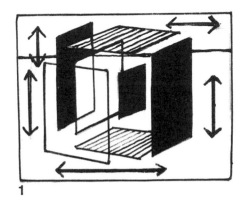

1

1. The split facets of a cube will help illustrate pictorial depth. These oblique angles are turned *at an angle to the picture plane*. They are not drawn in perspective but provide a sensation of recession. The artist controls the design made by the sensation of space—the going back—as well as the design on the flatness of his picture plane.

If you grasp the implications of this theory the business of "thrusts," "movements," "tensions" and such terminology used in describing pictorial dynamics will be easily understood. The over-all assembling of these pictorial elements provides unity and harmony to both figurative and abstract work. Where the "decorative" takes over in abstract painting and a work of art begins is often debatable.

2. The right hand side of the split cube has been taken as a starting point for the small design made in several grays, black and white. Over-lappings and flattening of some areas provide space illusions, some recession and negative space. Such experiments are valuable to obtain an understanding of abstract modulations of a simple kind.

Contrast this figure with the illustration of the Constructivist painting by Thépot on page 16. Here all depth has been cancelled out and the varied tones of gray lie flat to the picture plane with no recession allowed. Think of the Mondrian paintings where this always applies, or many contemporary works that insist upon the undisturbed flatness of the composition.

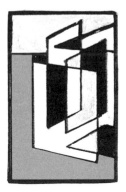

Negative and Positive Space

Negative space. This is the space surrounding the objects and must be considered in its relation to positive forms. We think of it as being flat to the picture plane and visually not dynamic or *positive*. The artist learns to pit the two against each other. Forms outside objects are fused and interlocked with positive volumes. The Cézanne still life on page 46 shows the carefully planned fusion of volumes on a flat surface. The design is closely knit—the composition planned *on the surface and in depth.*

If we can grasp this simplified defining of a complex subject—pictorial space—much that has hitherto been a mystery to us becomes clarified. Why, for example, Cézanne's "constructions after nature" please our eye by blending orderly Cubistic spatial forms with an intense sensitivity to the natural forms and colors of nature. The later Cubist experiments will be understood also and the steps to contemporary use of space in abstraction seem a logical progression.

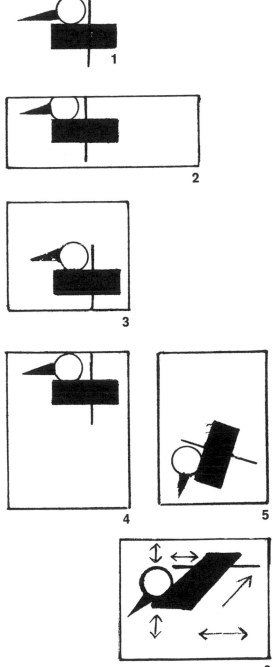

The Format

One of the considerations with which every artist must be concerned when beginning his picture is the format. Its shape—long, square, vertical, whatever its proportion—is a determining factor and decides what he places upon it. Experienced painters know this and spend considerable time weighing up the blank surface of their canvas for its compositional possibilities *before* they begin to paint, because they know that the horizontal and vertical containing lines of their format control pictorially how the elements to be placed on the surface will function. The naturalistic painter is very conscious of this and the "Golden Cut" or "Golden Section"—a line geometrically planned which cuts the rectangle into two divisions horizontally—was used and still is by many landscape painters who cherish the value of perfect relative proportions. This division supposedly gives us the exact point on which to draw a horizon line that does not divide our space into dull symmetrical proportions. Dynamic Symmetry is a complex geometric development of this theory which many artists still use to build an aesthetically harmonious grid of structural shapes and lines on which to erect their paintings or drawings.

Using a simple figure such as that shown in Diagram 1, we can see what happens when we surround it with various boundaries. Space filling, a major part of the artist's job, can be a sensitive operation. In much abstract work it becomes *the* problem, for upon it the painter puts his dependence on impact, color and significant expression. With obvious subject matter removed —the house, the tree, the figure—the formal values of organized space are all that he has left to make his work significant.

Observation of the figure in Diagrams 2, 3, 4 and 5 will give the clue to the many visual sensations made by moving the figure within varied boundaries. Size indications change, the sense of surrounding space diminishes or increases and with it the "feel" of satisfactory or unsatisfactory visual reaction. Paint these up on a large canvas and the sensation will be much more apparent. All figures are painted flat to the picture surface with no indication of deep or shallow recession behind the figure.

In Diagram 6, we have tilted the black accented rectangle to an oblique angle. Immediately we have a sense of recession, of a thrust into recessive space. The circle remains *flat* to the picture plane as does the horizontal line.

Such elementary dynamics are obvious, but it is unbelievable how many students are quite unaware of the importance of such controls and of how their work suffers as a result.

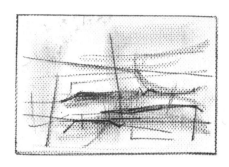

Developing the Composition

1. A scribble similar to Figure 1 jotted down from a panorama of mountainous country may be the beginning of a canvas. The opposing diagonals against the long horizontal lines are trees perhaps or telephone poles. The break-up of space into a structural pattern comes before the details of color, texture, and so on are added.

2. Similarly, the non-objective painter faces the canvas and begins to enliven the surface with lines, movements and shapes. Unmindful of the mountains, sky or trees, he may begin his work without recourse to subject matter. The excitement of inventing new relationships of lines and rhythms is sufficient inspiration for him. From such small drawings, he may develop his final work, taking it to completion with color and textural surfaces.

3. The first free lines may suggest tonal arrangements in black and white or demand a full color orchestration.

4. A typical shorthand note from a still life group which falls somewhere between the Abstract and figurative. Such notes are useful to the artist who has trained himself to see beyond the cold visual facts to the pictorial possibilities of his material.

5. A small oil panel made from nature, "The Bank of the Seine." Broad brushings of light and dark patterns.

MEXICAN STILL LIFE by Leonard Brooks.

Compositions within compositions. Choosing new arrangements from sections of your own finished paintings is a useful practice that will aid your compositional abilities. This can be done by cutting differently proportioned areas from cardboard and placing them over your paintings. Move these about until you find a composition that pleases you both in design and color content. Often simpler, stronger and more effective arrangements will suggest themselves, and these can be the start of a new painting. The detail shown at the right is a small area of the painting above isolated to demonstrate how an over-busy composition can be redeemed, its essence revealed. This method will work equally well with semi-figurative or abstract paintings.

1. Repetition of vertical and horizontal lines, the simplest repeat of a unit in time.

Elementary Principles of Design

Such terms as contrast, interval, alternation, rhythm, balance, unity within variety, repetition, symmetrical and asymmetrical, pattern and composition—all of these elements which go to make up the traditional formal design theories are still very much apparent and revealed constantly in the work of contemporary painters. Design has been spoken of as a "synonym of form" (Ralph Pearson); design in painting exists when the painting is complete as a unit and finished. Every element—line, mass, color, texture—has contributed its part to the whole and the sum of all elements placed in the fully functioning relationship at its highest point of integrated dominance by the artist. Then we say, to put it more simply, that "the picture works." We instinctively feel this is so, even though perhaps we do not know why and could not pin it down in words or separate all the disparate elements of pictorial feeling and knowledge that have been used in the final complexity of the work.

The wide-awake art student is constantly alive to design in nature and in the handwork of others, not only in painting but in the fine forms of handicraft and architecture, for here will be found the specialized world of design applied to other problems than that of painting. Sculpture, fine pottery, industrial design, and beyond these, the world of poetry, literature and music. Design and form is inherent in all of them and will enrich the artist's inner understanding of what creative "form" and the magic of "design" may embrace.

2. The repetition broken and interest added by off-beat spacing of lines.

3. Curved forms contrast with varied angular lines.

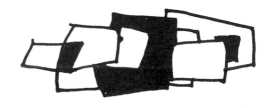

4. The black form dominates the cluster of white squared forms.

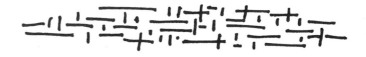

5. Dots and lines please our sense of pattern.

38

6. Rhythm of assorted shapes flow across the page.

7. Broken contrasts and agitations suggest dynamic force.

ON THE RIVER by Paul Klee. McNay Art Institute, San Antonio, Texas. The "line takes a walk." A drawing that uses the magic of line to suggest elements from a river journey. A hieroglyphic statement of an almost primitive kind. Boat, trees, shore—all are drawn in a flat calligraphic scrawl with much sophistication beneath the child-like technique. "To make memories abstract" was his stated purpose.

STUDIO INTERIOR

RIVER BANK

REFLECTIONS

Three sketches from actual scenes, made on small panels.
These show the first analytical transposition from the subject. Such material is absorbed and used later in all-out
abstract motifs.

Chiaroscuro

Light and shade and its treatment in a picture was much valued by the early figure painters. Rembrandt was the supreme exponent of the use of light and dark balance in expressive painting. The Abstract painter depends greatly on the skillful use of tonal dynamics to give life to his paintings.

Sculptors working in relief or full dimension use the contrasts and shadings of light on form and space to bring their works to life and many lessons can be learned from the study of sculpture or the actual modelling of form by the painter, using clay or other material for experiment.

The twelfth-century "Eve" shown here is the work of Gislebertus, a genius who worked for years beautifying the church in Autun, France. (*Gislebertus, Sculpture of Autun.*) It is a splendid example of the masterly use of decoration in relief carved in stone to form a work of art. Photographed and shown in the flat, its light and dark pattern emerges in rhythmic and magnificent counter-point.

The artist finds many enticing arrangements awaiting him in nature, and the delights of noting down black-and-white patterns suggestive of development into paintings are constantly surprising him. On the next page, there is a drawing made from a basket of pears on a table. Charcoal and white crayons were used, color was forgotten and only the many tones of grays, blacks and whites noted (Figure 1). The modelling of the forms is emphasized with a strong lighting effect of highlights and shadows.

At a later date, the curved forms were used in a near-square composition based on the material made in the drawing study. Color was added, but the initial conception of strong contrasting chiaroscuro was used in developing the Semi-Abstraction (Figure 2).

The transposition from color to black and white in a photograph is often a shock to the painter who finds that though the picture is successful in color it does not seem to be so in black-and-white tones. It is an interesting way for a beginner to see his paintings translated into another dimension. Frequently his canvas is improved by such a change, or a photograph will suggest a new interpretation.

EVE. Photograph by Franceschi.

1

A casein painting using a complex tonal scheme derived from a seashore motif.

Wash drawing by Harold Black. Uses many tones of grays and black and white to form a composition derived from plant forms.

2

Transposition

1. A detail from an oil painting made as a careful realistic study of tone and color. In it, the light and dark tones were carefully observed. It is used here to show several other ways in which we may wish to interpret and transpose the subject for more dynamic and imaginative picture making.

2. The flat outline considered. Such line drawing using an even hard edge around the objects allows us to consider the flat surfaces, the positive and negative spaces.

3. The volumes studied. Here the weight and bulk of the object is examined with the planes sharply defined by dark accents.

4. The objects freed from visual reality. Here we extract the planes and volumes we wish to use and reassemble them in a new order at our own discretion. We strive for a sense of order, balance and a visual completeness. Distortions and changes of shapes are made if need be. We may show several sides, a number of viewpoints of the same object in the same picture—a multiple view—if we require it. The rules of perspective and literal representation are disregarded.

5. A final step that bears little relation to the actual subject yet is derived from it. This is a quick abstract note made from memory of the subject. A few of the major movements of line and form are recollected. Such a note is dug up from memory at a later date, free from literal representation but influenced by previous analysis and study of the subject.

FORMALISM

A New Classicism

Most art historians agree that Cézanne, the "Master of Aix," was the father of modern art. Perhaps van Gogh and Gauguin are better known to the world through the popularization of their works in books and movies which have romanticized their difficult lives, but Cézanne, the quiet and retiring hermit who lived from 1839 to 1906 and worked in comparative obscurity for most of his life as a painter, was the man destined to influence the twentieth-century world of art more than any other artist of his time. To him, we look for the basic understandings on which modern painting began. Today, many of his pronouncements and theories are considered tame and frequently scholars and researchers have developed the theories far beyond what Cézanne himself may have imagined. Nevertheless, to understand the later manifestations of abstraction, we must look to Cézanne and his work to trace the steps toward the painting of today.

Gradually the Cézanne theory emerges and his work becomes stamped with the unmistakable signs of a giant personality masked under the quiet, shy and stubborn manner. To Cézanne, working quietly through the influences of the Impressionists and their search for ways to capture light and atmosphere, the path seemed clear and obvious. Beginning with a thick opulent impasto of paint, Cézanne soon refined his painting technique to a thin controlled series of touches that would capture for him what he called "his little sensation before Nature." Significant form, the search for the basic structural essence, the architecture of the form underlying the object would redeem for him the feeling that painting had lost its way, that it had gone astray and could only be saved by bringing

THE POPLARS by Monet (1891). The Metropolitan Museum of Art. Bequest of Mrs. H. O. Havemeyer, 1927, The H. O. Havemeyer Collection. The effect of light, lyrical and poetic depiction of trees against the sky in rough impastos of flickering touches of paint. A modern feeling of division of the square space is created by the repetitional verticals of the tree trunks.

VILLAGE OF GARDANNE by Cézanne. In the Brooklyn Museum Collection. Structural build-up of volumes and concern for spatial organization is evident here. The contrast of soft and broken edges, the definite and considered brush strokes to mould forms, the searching strokes of the first drawing-in—all of these reveal the Cézanne manner of building up his canvases.

back a new classicism founded on the great art of the past.

He felt that Impressionism with its hazy indefiniteness of shape must be re-invigorated and underlying form and structure emphasized. The picture must be organized with controlled planes, recession and depth, color made organic, an integral part of the language of form, not something to be added to the forms as an afterthought. The picture would find its own equilibriums drawn from deep sources of a sensitive eye in front of nature's endless storehouse of shapes, colors and forms. The constructive and geometrical harmony of such paintings would reveal the essential truths of natural forms, unlocking their secrets in the rhythmic progressions and relations selected and transposed from the objects themselves. This, of course, is a classic concept but with added modern overtones.

In addition to his search for structure, Cézanne pursued his experiments in how color could be synonymous with form and could in itself suggest depth and volumes. All this kept him busy before his easel for a lifetime, working incessantly in spite of much disregard and neglect from most of his contemporaries until his last years.

STILL LIFE—PEACHES by Renoir.
The Metropolitan Museum of Art.
Bequest of Stephen C. Clark.

The contrast between structural seeing and the soft, broken touches of the Impressionists is clearly revealed in these two paintings by two masters of the still life. A close scrutiny of the original canvases will demonstrate how Cézanne's search for a "modulating" technique brought into being his use of controlled planes and edges, emphasis of picture plane and concern for positive and negative space.

STILL LIFE—APPLES AND PEARS
by Cézanne.
The Metropolitan Museum of Art.
Bequest of Stephen C. Clark.

Cubism

We have noted how Cézanne developed a way of seeing that eliminated much of the accidental and ephemeral in his subjects, whether still life, figure or landscape. From 1907 to 1912 Picasso and Braque, both young and vigorous, were producing paintings carrying Cézanne's ideas to the extreme. They gave up the representation of objects as they appeared, to discover the inherent construction underlying them. It was the geometric quality of the first paintings by Braque that gave the name to the movement when a critic wrote, "He mistreats form, reduces everything, sites, figures and houses, to geometric outlines, to cubes." Thus the word "Cubism" was born.

Art historians break down the main Cubist movements into three periods. In the first period the geometric and underlying forms were stressed. The second was the fracturing of the forms with multiple seeing. The third period, the synthetic type, a re-organization of geometric elements (1912 to 1914), liberated form in new and imaginative combinations.

Cubism was essentially a method that allowed the artist to unite and tie together unrelated elements in a composition. It freed the artist from the confines of copying outlines of exact visual forms while allowing him freedom to re-order and distort size and form to the dictates of his over-all

THE TABLE by Braque (1928). Collection, The Museum of Modern Art, New York. Acquired through the Lillie P. Bliss Bequest. This masterpiece in ochres, deep blues, browns and yellow marks a high point in Braque's exploration of space. Here the subject inspires him to a virtuosity of composition and use of Cubist distortion in "fracturing of the image."

ZIRCHOW V by Lyonel Feininger. In the Brooklyn Museum Collection. Cubist evaluation of landscape and architectural form. A well-knit study of interlocking planes and cube volumes made in the early years of Cubism when such paintings first shocked the traditional painters.

47

design. He could, if he wished, represent two or three images of what he sees—showing at the same time the circular rim of the cup from above as well as the profile of its shape. Planes could be tilted flat to the picture surface instead of using a visual perspective of receding lines; objects could be shown at different levels. The picture becomes a montage of viewpoints projected simultaneously on the canvas. Study the Braque painting reproduced on page 47.

Before the first World War, a host of followers took up the Cubist manner of working and satellite schools sprang up throughout Europe. Orphism, Purism, Section d'Or, and other groups flew the banner of Cubism. A long list of well-known names could be given here, drawn from France, Germany and other European countries: for example, Gleizes, Metzinger, Gris, Leger. In the United States, Feininger, Marin, Weber, and others were attracted to the Cubist painters' techniques.

Multiple images, fractured planes, a hundred facets breaking across paintings, such as "Ma Jolie" by Picasso, reproduced on page 50, showed the intense searching for spatial construction. Shadows, highlights, in-between tones, each turn of a form against another were noted and structuralized on the canvas. The result was justified by more knowledge, more inventions in the control of space, but the pictures came to be *over* modulated, busy with countless planes and forms, with dry and uninspired color schemes, and soon became too repetitious. The time came for a breakaway to new experiments, for there were new discoveries to be made. As in most extreme movements that begin with enthusiasm and spontaneity, there comes a moment when the fires need refuelling and a reassessment and revaluation of what has been accomplished is required.

Lhote, a Cubist of later years, says that the Cubists' sudden preoccupation with color, which infected many of their paintings in the later, unorthodox Cubism, was to establish a new fusion of elements. Formerly, the Cubists' preoccupation in the search for form had often excluded color in favor of geometric planes and facets in grays and browns. The new interest in color led to the more modern development of Cubist painting as practised by the outstanding Cubist painters of France: La Fresnaye, Villon, Lhote and others. In other words, now color masses and areas of color, overlined and defined with planes, lines and overwritings, were all unified and fused into a satisfying visual experience for the onlooker. Thus, color areas plus compositional line and planar projection to bind the loose areas of color together on the picture plane is the basis for much of our contemporary painting.

The Fractured Image. Semi-Abstraction is used in the paintings, shown opposite, to transpose the subject into a composition removed from literal seeing. Planes, recession into pictorial space, color, and texture combine to make the selected subject visually interesting as a painting. The figurative is the starting point, but the artist takes and leaves what he finds of value to him as a painter.

VENICE MORNING

WHITE PALACE

PEAR STILL LIFE

MEXICAN SPRING

STUDIO LIGHT

STILL LIFE

STILL LIFE by Roger de la Fresnaye (1914). Collection, The Museum of Modern Art, New York. Gift of Mrs. John D. Rockefeller, Jr. La Fresnaye, an admirer of Cézanne and influenced by Braque, forged a style of colorful Cubistic imagery. Illness dogged his maturity and prevented the full flowering of his genius.

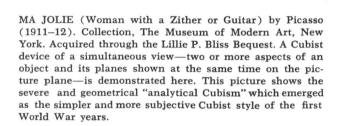

MA JOLIE (Woman with a Zither or Guitar) by Picasso (1911–12). Collection, The Museum of Modern Art, New York. Acquired through the Lillie P. Bliss Bequest. A Cubist device of a simultaneous view—two or more aspects of an object and its planes shown at the same time on the picture plane—is demonstrated here. This picture shows the severe and geometrical "analytical Cubism" which emerged as the simpler and more subjective Cubist style of the first World War years.

VIOLIN AND ENGRAVING by Juan Gris (1913). Collection, The Museum of Modern Art, New York. Bequest of Anna Erickson Levene. Analytical Cubism is used here to transpose a violin and still life into a heavily-textured collage combined with oil painting. An interesting treatment of Cubist technique.

FROZEN STATION by John Hultberg, (1958). Oil. Spatial forms are used for exciting movements in depth. Colorful areas move back and forth in an orchestrated symphony of form. Neither purely abstract nor figurative, a personal new world is created and the subject revealed to us in a new reality.

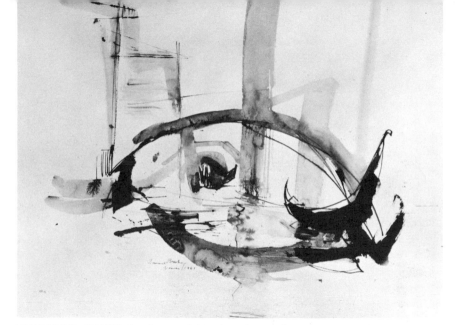

VENETIAN STUDY by Leonard Brooks. An exploratory drawing from nature that searches out pictorial elements of the image and "fractures" them into essential movements of line and mass.

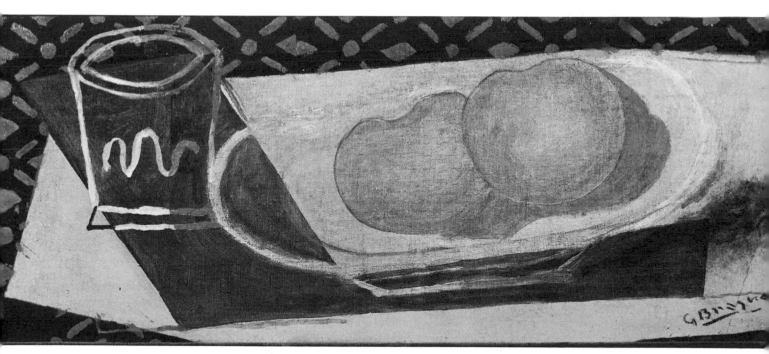

STILL LIFE by Braque. McNay Art Institute, San Antonio, Texas. A small panel of a decorative nature. Observe the simultaneous seeing of the straight bottom of the glass and the ellipse, and the use of light-dark outline for emphatic definition.

Above is a long decorative oil panel using bottle, fruit and plant forms in a horizontal design. Below, a small panel using the "Fractured Image" break-up of space from a still-life group is shown.

The Fractured Image

We have sketched briefly some of the background from which the abstract art movement emerged. In the bibliography are listed certain key books that expand in great detail these necessarily cursory remarks about the complexities of the vital periods during the early years of modern art.

To help our understanding, we will now lean toward the more practical aspects of drawing and painting in projects that will give us a more direct and deeper appreciation of some of the pictorial problems with which the contemporary painter is faced when he makes his expressive statements. By trying some of these exercises, the student may clarify for himself much that becomes over-complicated in words alone.

"The main thing is modelling; one shouldn't even say modelling, but modulating. . . ." said Cézanne.

Although Cézanne spoke of the geometric elements of cone, cylinder and sphere, these were used only as an aid to help him realize and transform natural objects into related paint surfaces spatially organized. He always began with nature, the inspiration for his delight and absorption in modulated color and formal constructions on his canvas.

We may study and explore this approach ourselves in a series of drawings from simple objects in our studio. Space modulation will be defined more clearly for us if we devote a morning to this problem. On pages 56 and 57 (Figures 1 to 5), we see the flattening out of three-dimensional forms and how they can be controlled by the use of horizontal and vertical planes.

STILL LIFE by James Pinto. A semi-abstract painting using the forms of fruit and table-top as a starting point for a composition. The rich tonal scheme uses curved forms against a linear pattern.

REBOZOS by Leonard Brooks.

Planes and Edges

The meeting of edges of the planes gives us the control of pictorial space. Sometimes these edges are very apparent in the objects to be drawn; at other times they are concealed or non-existent to the eye and we must feel the change of weight and volume, sensing the line that will define for us recession and space. Figure draftsmen are well aware of this and give solidity and construction to their figure drawings with well-defined structural lines, where none exist in the subject itself.

This emphasis on edges and geometric planes was the important contribution of Cézanne which the Cubists utilized in developing the Cubist theory.

As an example to some of the ways we may choose to reorder our material to more effective visual ends, I have set out an exercise that can be easily duplicated in your studio or workroom. All you need is a few objects of different shapes and contours and time to deliberate upon your way of interpreting the facts before you.

In approaching this divorce from the reality of the objects, a sketch could be made in simple line, tracing the all-over patterns and shapes of things as they are set out in their related places. Figure 1 is a quick pencil drawing of everything that happened to be in a corner of the room where I work. It puts down everything and leaves nothing out. Such drawings often have a charm of their own, for if they are not too photographically rendered, they have removed themselves one step from mere imitative seeing and already provide us with some mark of the artist's personality by using the limitations of line and dismissing the realistic tonal lights and darks of accidental lighting.

The next step is a more selective one. Larger forms are used, the eye moves closer and takes from the over-all group shapes and spaces that give the painter more opportunity for compositional seeing. This drawing was made in charcoal with some slight tonal suggestion combined wth outline. Diagonal and horizontal lines interlock the planes across the surface of the drawing and an effort is made to give varied sizes to the interlocking spaces. No attempt has been made to render exact accuracy of size and shape (Figure 2).

Figure 3 breaks free from the objects altogether. This is a more difficult step. One way of helping to free oneself from depicting literal fact at this stage is to turn one's back on the group and draw from memory, reassembling at will the elements that have been impressed on the mind. Brushes, a jug or jar, a bottle and table forms—draw these, using

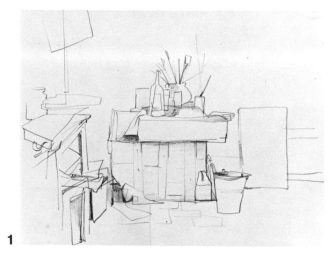

56

only the large rhythms and directional lines that indicate the flat and horizontal planes. This type of "fractured" cubism has some resemblance to the early Cubist analytical paintings.

Ink and brush were used in the next drawing (Figure 4). Here the forms are freed from the more formal controls of the charcoal drawing. Planes are flattened out, and space and depth flattened by strong use of vertical and horizontal lines stressing the flat character of the plane on which the drawing is made. It is obvious here that the group has become only an excuse for making a black-and-white drawing, which is exciting as a drawing *not* because of the story the objects tell; subject matter is secondary to the drawing itself.

The final part of our exercise, Figure 5, was made with collage and some drawing with ink and brush over the various papers assembled on a colored background. (See the chapter on Paper and Rags, page 106.) Newspapers and vari-textured papers are cut and pasted down forming planes and areas that move in overlapping space. Curves and straight lines are drawn to develop a design that seems to form a satisfactory pattern. Here we have reached the point where we could, if we are talented and have luck, make a picture that will work for us. If you wish to take it further, now is the time to select a color scheme and to start your canvas. Take the colors from the actual objects if

4

5

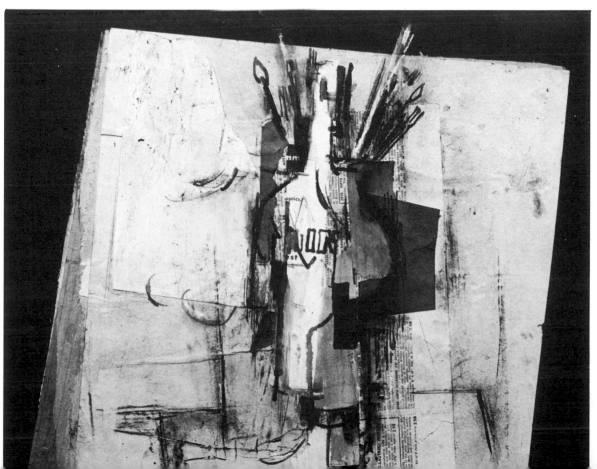

Two motifs taken from a cluttered corner of the studio. Note how the shapes of the objects are fused into the surrounding shapes. The play of light and the variation of edges help the fusion of new relationships of form and the transposition from factual objects.

1. An oil painting made in a literal way from a still life group. The subject has been studied for tonal and color accuracy and is treated in an Impressionistic painting technique.

2. A study in heavy line from the same group isolating the main movements, accents and linear pattern. An excellent way to break away from a too literal rendering in the approach to semi-abstraction.

3. A small sketch in pencil to analyze the planes and volumes of the objects. Here the fracturing of objects into simple flat planes is obvious. The placing of varied light and dark areas is also studied before beginning an actual painting. Such a method of study is useful before beginning a "Fractured Image" painting similar to Figure 4.

4. "Sunflower Still Life." This painting was made from a series of such studies from the realistic to the transposed version. It is shown here in its finished form after textures, color and final disposition of objects in space had been considered.

you wish, the grays and whites of the spaces around the objects, the green bottle, the yellow brushes. Or select an arbitrary scheme, limiting yourself to a few warm tones, a touch of orange and black and white. (Figure 5 is reproduced in color on page 61.)

If you try a few exercises of this type you will soon find that working in the Cubist technique is not quite as easy as it may appear at first sight. You will be anxious to go back and take another look at the Gris and Picasso paintings, which seemed to be put together so casually and without much effort or struggle. Their subtle distortions and fracturings will make more sense to you after you have tried to do some multiple seeing yourself.

Undoubtedly you will have a new respect for and a greater understanding of the problems the Cubists set for themselves in their first experiments.

Having done a number of analytical studies where you have concentrated on searching for basic forms and structural and spatial compositions, you will find, if such a direction is new to you, that your previous work may look "flabby" and perhaps "boneless." Faults in composition will be more apparent and you may feel the urge to redo and reconstruct your earlier efforts. When you try another painting, the training your eye and mind has had in seeing through the external object to basic picture making will be evident.

Ruler and Compass

Modern art is a river rampant with forceful currents and changes of direction and has many tributaries. In tracing its course we will find there is no clear cleavage of aim and direction. Characteristic styles overlap, absorb each other; new impetus often swells from an outgoing tide.

Following the impact of the Cubist revolution, we see groups of painters extracting the "neo-plastic" essence, that is, the use of purely geometric and structural formations shorn of all accidental qualities, disciplined and sharply conceived. To many of us, these may seem too much so; the dry unemotional assembling of precise lines in restricted color by Mondrain, the cold, uncompromising surfaces of the Constructivists who will have nothing of the freely conceived work of the Expressionists may seem uninteresting. For the formalist painter, however, the sense of rigid order and clean control architecturally conceived becomes a new reality.

Springing from Cubist origins, the spirit of

→

Six formal exercises of a varied nature which may suggest similar experimental projects of your own. For the exercises suggested here use a 16 by 20 inch format; use oil, pastel or casein with sufficient textural brushwork to vary areas. Observe changes in edges where light spaces meet other spaces. At times these will be "hard," sharply defined, often they will demand "soft" lost edges of definition. There is no rule to guide you in the emphasis of paint stroke against paint stroke but you will soon sense when such edges define space for you and seem to "feel" right. Work from large, blocked-out areas to refinement of small space break-up, leaving the detailed touches to the last, *after* the big design is indicated. Try to relate all lines and flat forms to the edges of the shape you are filling. Note that "Abstract Oval" uses diagonal and curved lines to form a design within an elliptical space. Do not copy what is shown here but use similar lines to form your own pattern. "Vertical Blue" uses only vertical and diagonal lines. Again choose your own break-up of space. Both these exercises will be rewarding in understanding the shape of a totally abstract semi-formalist painting, if carried through with thought and sensitivity to the problem at hand. The development of "Bottle and Brushes" is described on pages 56 and 57. The other exercises shown use some of the different approaches we have considered in this book. Pastel, oil, collage—all of these are used in combination or alone. A series of small experiments of this kind, breaking away from your usual way of working, can be very enlightening. Use the abstract alphabet (see page 96) to suggest new ways of composing and painting.

COMPOSITION by Piet Mondrian (1925). Collection, The Museum of Modern Art, New York. Gift of Philip C. Johnson. The founder of Neo-Plasticism, endlessly searching for the perfection of simplicity, here reduces the canvas to five flat colored areas. Contrast this painting, such formal division of line and space, with the enriched textured movements of the canvases of Expressionists such as Kandinsky, who were also working at this time.

ABSTRACT OVAL

VERTICAL BLUE

YELLOW AND BLACK

RED AND WHITE

BOTTLE AND BRUSHES

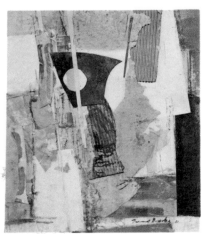

MUSIC PANEL

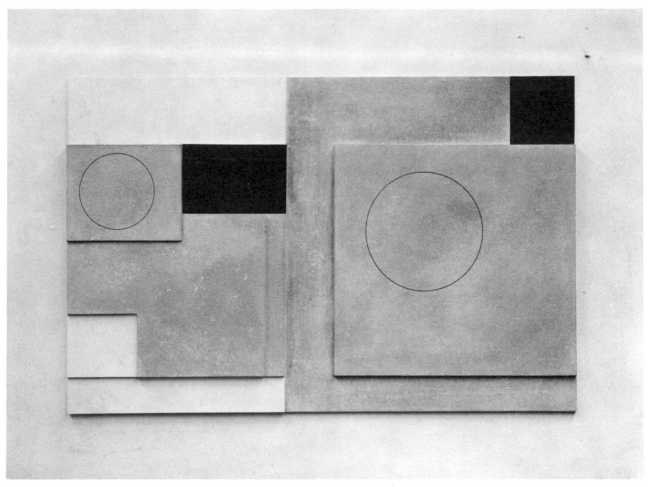

RELIEF by Ben Nicholson (1939). Collection, The Museum of Modern Art, New York. Gift of H. S. Ede and the artist. Perhaps the best known British Abstractionist, Nicholson's reliefs in geometric and austere patterns spring from the Neo-Plasticists' and Constructivists' approach. A study in controlled formalism.

CORDOBA by Luc Peire (1960).

de Stijl (the Style) in Holland and of artists like Malevitch in Russia, the Constructivist movement has become an important branch of contemporary painting, a steadily growing influence in the present day world of scientific and technological living. These Neo-Plastic artists and others of the Bauhaus movement in Germany helped form our modern concepts of design in daily living, changing the forms of architecture through men like Gropius, Saarinen and others.

All this has cleared the way for men like inventor-designer R. Buckminster Fuller who has discovered in contemporary pattern and design a miraculous world of engineering and architectural wonder in his "geodesic dome."

Many serious painters have appeared in the younger generation of Europeans to continue the tradition of Constructivism. In the United States, there is much interest in such well-known men as Albers, Gabo, Calder, Pevsner and others who work formally in a geometric manner.

The question is too large to discuss here in detail, but the interested student will soon find himself enmeshed in many Constructivist theories.

The history of formalism in its many ramifications is a long one and plenty of relevant material awaits your reading. Many of the painters who turned from Expressionism and its emotional frenzies were highly literate, fond of issuing manifestos and credos about their intentions and work, and the literature they produced is direct and to the point. Mondrian's essay *Plastic Art and Pure Plastic Art* expounds his theories. The letters, notes and essays of such men as Masson, Klee, Gris, Kandinsky and others will provide much fascinating study to the interested student and artist. These are notes made by the painters themselves, not by the critics who came afterwards, and they are valuable as records made at the time of production, often before the painter was established or well-known. Most of these painters with a geometric bias express themselves well in words to explain their aesthetic and spiritual aims. Gabo has said, "By means of constructive techniques today we are able to bring to light forces hidden in nature and to realize psychological effects . . . We do not turn away from nature but, on the contrary, we penetrate her more profoundly than naturalistic art ever was able to do."

Some of the lessons to be learned from the Constructivist approach will be apparent if we try an elementary assignment which may help us to understand the value as well as the techniques of this important aspect of contemporary painting.

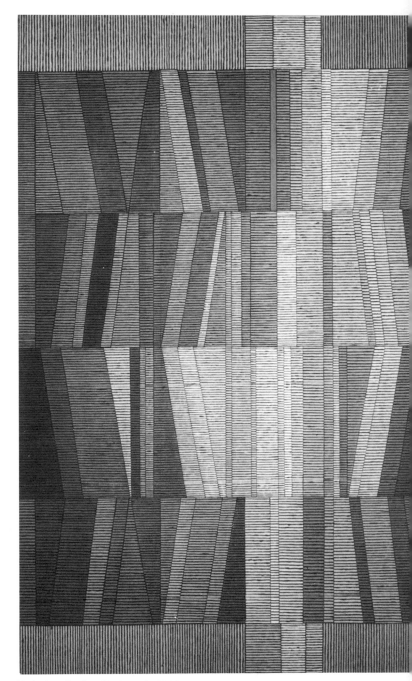

Painting by Leo Breuer (1962).

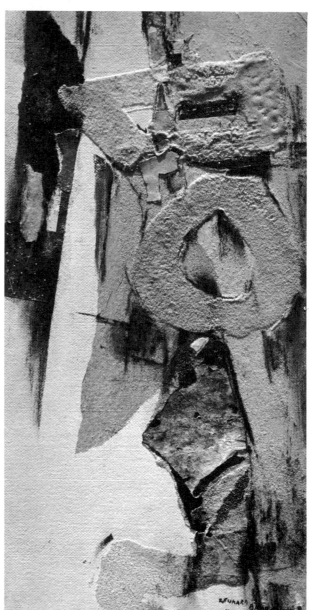

Assignment in Formalism

1. The clean-cut edges of a number of geometrical shapes are cut at random. Limit these to four shapes. Choose a variety of tones, black to white. Select a format of rectangular shape. Assemble these as you will, shifting them about until you are satisfied with their placing. Paste them on their background.

2. Use the design you have made for a larger *painted* interpretation. Use a mat gouache or casein paint and choose two or three values in a limited range of monochromatic color, for example a dark brown, two or three lightened versions (with white) of the same brown, and a white. Paint on a 20 by 16 inch illustration board, trying to make a cleanly formal and even presentation of all washes of pigment. Use a broad flat brush and mix a batch of sufficient color for each section of the painting, applying it smoothly from top to bottom.

Try this in smaller versions of one brilliant color—a yellow perhaps—and two or three grays. Try it in a complementary scheme of opposites, one bright red and two or three greens, an orange and violet in grayed form.

The actual exercising of a disciplined manner of working may seem strange to you if you are accustomed to the freedoms and nervous brushings of "free" painting, but the experience will be a curious and perhaps enlightening one. It will help you understand the beauty inherent in the flat unagitated surface of paint, especially if you have contrived a satisfying spatial design before adding color.

3. Using the same simple basic forms as in the paper-cut experiment, circles and diagonals are put together in a mixed technique panel. Instead of flat color, varied textures are added made with paint and sand pastes formed with polymer resin. This step, a semi-formalist design, still uses geometrical elements but in a looser, freer style.

Black-and-white rendering by Michel Seuphor. Creates a
formalist world with precise linear space and tones.

Gouache by Roger-François Thépot. A finely rendered study by a French Constructivist made in a highly geometrical style far removed from representation.

Collage by Leonard Brooks. Many textures are utilized in an experimental collage of semi-formal nature. Strong contrasts of white, black, and gray are used.

EXPRESSIONISM

In the foregoing pages we suggested trying some Cubist techniques and we have studied a few of the elements of formalism and the Constructivist approach to picture making. Now we are ready to look over the other side of the fence, to pay another visit to our friends in studio number two where the paint flew thick and heavy, which we visited earlier.

Before we do so, and before we try a few experiments ourselves in free gestures of "action-painting," let us glance briefly over the history of the first modern Expressionists as well as Abstract Expressionism as it exists today.

Expressionism in its real sense has always been with us, for all expressive painting has this quality. Emotionalism is a quality to be found in many early works—El Greco is a good example, or Grünewald. Modern expressionism came into being with the work of men such as van Gogh, Munch and Ensor at the beginning of the twentieth century. It is a strongly subjective personal vision which uses strong contrasts and highly-colored dramatic visions of an obsessive and powerful kind. Symbolic expressionism, romantic expressionism, the social realism of Mexico, the short-lived

QUALM by James Brooks (1954). Collection, The Museum of Modern Art, New York. Gift of Mrs. Bliss Parkinson. Large curved areas, a strongly contrasted color and tonal pattern with each brush mark sensitively "gestured" against the other gives this finely painted abstraction its fascination and completeness.

MONT VALERIEN by Maurice de Vlaminck (1903). Collection, The Museum of Modern Art, New York. Acquired through the Lillie P. Bliss Bequest. An early example of Vlaminck's Fauve period—brilliant in color and frantic in brush stroke, influenced by van Gogh. This phase lasted until 1907 when he painted his last Fauve canvas and turned to the theories of Cézanne. Six years later he deserted Cézannism for the sadness of his Expressionistic black skies, snowy streets, and flower subjects, done in thickly impastoed swirls of paint.

Regional schools of the United States expressing the dilemma of the depression years, the war years' pictures of protest—including Picasso's "Guernica" —all of these are samples of the many forms of Expressionist art. All of them are figurative, though the degree of inventive distortion and semi-abstraction is limitless. Cubist means are sometimes incorporated in the techniques, or an amalgam of Impressionist color and Cézanne theory is added to a strong hard-edged outline used to provide strength and impact. Gauguin and Munch tried many such combinations in their work, and Chagall is worth studying for this aspect of assimilated techniques with added personal subject matter.

In 1905, a short-lived but influential school of painters emerged called the Fauves . . . the "Wild Beasts." These men, Matisse, Derain, Vlaminck and Dufy, painted the lively and sensuous interpretations of life about them in France with passionate reaction to the scene. Flowers, still life, landscapes and figures blazed with color in a decorative and wild fury of thick paint and emotional force. The group soon dispersed but the impact of brilliant hues and joyful vivid painting broke with the realistic study of Impressionist light and released the imagination in a shower of paintings based on a dynamic sensualism. Chiaroscuro was forgotten, space construction in areas of flat and bright colors with sharp defining lines was used and a "condensation of sensation" helped the painter to transpose his subject, free from details and realistic matter that did not contribute to the over-all impact and immediate sensation of the artist's feelings.

Braque and others soon moved on from this manner of working. Cubism, with its orderly controls brought about the statement by Braque that "he liked the rule which corrected the emotion." The split that was later to take painters into the two separate schools of thought in the world of Abstract Art was already in evidence. The emotional freedoms of the Fauves were to be reconsidered, controlled, scattered and realigned into many different camps. But painting, freed from nineteenth century concepts by the short revolution, would never be the same again.

The Image Forsaken

When a painter named Kandinsky said in Germany, about 1911, that "objects harmed his pictures" he stated a conviction that has become today a dictum for many serious and world-renowned creative painters. The first consternation and bewilderment caused by Kandinsky's work which followed on his discovery has been forgotten and in most places where pictures are collected and gathered as historical documents of the changing aspects of the modern movement in painting, Kandinsky's work is paramount and dominant. He was the first real leader of what was to be a gigantic revolt against the way of painting and seeing that had ruled the artist since the times of the Renaissance.

IMPROVISATION NO. 27 by Wassily Kandinsky (1912). The Metropolitan Museum of Art. The Alfred Stieglitz Collection, 1949. The title provides the clue. An improvisation using a series of shapes, lines, and beautiful color in a freely expressed inventive manner, long antedating the Abstract Expressionists of fifty years later. An early style which led Kandinsky to his more formal and geometric later period.

CAMDEN MOUNTAIN ACROSS THE BAY by John Marin (1922). Collection, The Museum of Modern Art, New York. Gift of Mrs. John D. Rockefeller, Jr. A calligraphic statement from nature by a master watercolorist. A deceptively simple and exuberant brushing puts down the sweep of a panorama. A summing up and transposing done directly with a lively brush, from fact to inspired painting.

As a teacher in 1903, he had already absorbed the Impressionist theory and painted palette knife paintings influenced by Monet. This was followed by a period of Fauvism, but by 1910 he was deep in the excitement of his first Non-Objective abstract works. Looking at these today, especially his first abstract watercolors, we see a curious relation to some of the free Abstract Expressionist works of today. His insistence on separating the objects and forms of nature from the inventions and elements of "the inner desire of the subject which determines its form" is very much part of the creed of the Vitalist group today. In his middle period, Kandinsky turned more and more to a formalist pattern in his work eliminating many of the free calligraphic scrawls and writings of his first period.

The straight line and circle together with carefully conceived and modulated color harmonies gives an architectural feeling to his work contrasting with the explosive and dynamic force of his abstract beginnings. His inventive spirit has produced a body of work that has yet to be properly evaluated. His name is less known, for example, than Picasso's except in the circles of artists and collectors, but his contribution to modern paintings may well be, when weighed in the near future, of considerably more value to artists living and working in this agitated and mechanical space age, for his idiom is nearer to the needs of our times. The combination of spiritual and pure plastic values may be the recipe needed for progressive work and the creative continuity of the next cycle of painting.

Oil Painting by Marcelle Ferron (1958).

Two examples of The Image Forsaken—the Formal and the Free period. Here we see how color and design can deliver their own impact in entirely different ways. Marcelle Ferron, left, uses free exuberant spatula work. Brilliant reds, blues, greens and mauves sparkle in the dragged and broken paint textures against the white background. Evocative of nature, the painting creates a new world of flower-like form and color. Detailed and exquisite technical control give the Luc Peire painting, below, fine finish typical of Constructivists' work. Within the limited means allowed, this painter produces startling variations of color and controlled spatial compositions. His present work evolved from early Expressionist Belgian painting to the clean controlled formalism of his style today.

MANOLETE by Luc Peire (1957). Oil. Collection Musée Communal des Beaux Arts, Bruges.

GARDEN IN SOCHI by Arshile Gorky (1941). Collection, The Museum of Modern Art, New York. Gift of Wolfgang S. Schwacher. A personal symbolism using freely Surrealistic forms in a rich tonal composition. Such organic abstraction is in the full stream of contemporary trends.

SEATED WOMAN by Picasso (1926-27). Collection, The Museum of Modern Art. Strong linear drawing and flat contrasting color enliven this phase of Picasso experiment. Compare this with earlier many-faceted Cubist paintings.

1

2

4

3

5

6

A Group of Techniques

Some technical means are shown on the opposite page. Six small color abstractions demonstrate a few of the techniques much used in contemporary nonfigurative painting.

1. Direct palette knife strokes of oil paint applied without dilutants or medium. A lively impasto of "broken" color *(two or three colors not overmixed until the color goes dead),* each color retaining much of its own pure hue. A technique beloved by Tachist painters.

2. Extra-thick plastic cement base is used to build up heavy impastos for glazing and painting (when dry). Underpainting quick-drying white is often used, but for extreme textures, pastes or cements are usually preferred. Make these pastes with white glue and celite (ground up sea shells) or with marble dusts and fine sands. Certain builders' cements are used by some artists. Experiment in order to find what is permanent and suitable.

3. Thin stain of diluted oil paint in the form of a glaze brushed over white ground or thick underpainting white. This gives a glow to the color. Contrasting opaque strokes of thicker paint applied with palette knife or brush build up the forms.

4. Wax crayon drawing on paper with watercolor and casein paint over the wax—rich textural effects can be made with this technique. Try the same with wax and overlays of India ink. After the ink has dried, wash it away under the tap and use this textured base for casein painting to finish the painting in opaque touches.

5. Traditional brush work using oil on white canvas. A thin staining "drawing-in" first, thicker paint brushed over this with controlled brush-work using bristle or sable brushes. An ideal technique for controlled and well-planned abstract work. Such workmanlike and beautifully executed technique are still much practiced by the "School of Paris" painters.

6. Broad spatula strokes of oil paint applied freely and thickly to cut large textured shapes against each other. Different widths of metal stripping, used as spatulas, or a number of house-painters' putty knives will be found valuable for this technique.

Painting by Leonard Brooks

Abstract Expressionism

The naming and classification of art movements is an arbitrary interpretation at the best of times and it is not without point that the Dadaists named their movement in 1916 by the capricious act of sticking a pin, held by a blindfolded member, into a dictionary to emphasize the accidental nature of their society.

Abstract Expressionism is the name that has been used to describe the work of some recent American painters but the definition is a loose one because many of the works of painters often exhibited together as Abstract Expressionists are disparate and far from similar in manner or intent. The technique of Abstract Expressionism is generally based on free and automatic "action painting." Nothing interposes itself between the gesture of painting and the artist. The painter allows the brush and color to give expression (of an abstract kind) to his feelings and emotions. Sometimes the idea and statement to be revealed

FANTASIA IN BLUE by Hans Hofmann, (1954). Collection of Whitney Museum of American Art, New York. Strong contrasts, vigorous and exciting brushwork and textures by a veteran Abstractionist who has influenced the American scene. A staccato theme vibrant in blues and whites.

SONG OF ESTHER by Abraham Rattner (1958). Collection of Whitney Museum of American Art, New York. Strongly expressionistic color and form beautifully controlled, from large forms to smallest modulation of color in the lesser forms. A "painter's painting" that is worth much study.

SEA AND WIND by Leonard Brooks. A shore-and-sea motif uses free technique to suggest the movement and force of wind and wave.

is conceived before painting, but as often as not the spontaneous gesture and "engagement" before the canvas generates its own energies and conclusions.

This, like most techniques in painting, is not new. Anyone who has watched a traditional Japanese artist whirl a large brush in a flashing stroke over a large screen to form beautiful calligraphy or a bamboo leaf has seen a similar free gesture. The loose blobs and freely brushed strokes of the large, well-known Monet water-lily panels are almost as recklessly applied and for that matter so are the brilliant stabs of watercolor on a Turner

or Sargent sketch. The main difference is, of course, whether or not in the final result such energy has or has not produced an image. In the case of the Abstract Expressionist the painting *itself* becomes the theme. Unlike the paintings of the Cubists who took the subject and re-vitalized it by new ways of seeing, the Abstract Expressionist generally begins without a preconceived image— the strokes and textures and colors become the subject. Sir Herbert Read speaks of ". . . another kind of image, not an associated pictorial image, but a sensational image, an image of an indeterminate shape and imprecise colors, which perhaps comes from a deeper layer of the unconscious, with no immediate perceptual associations from the external world." He related this image with the work of Jackson Pollock whose twirls and ropings of overlapping paints and enamels dripping liberally over yards of canvas evoked new and powerful visual sensations during the forties.

These accidental rhythms and color modulations seemed to breathe a life of their own. The directing hand became nebulous, the "interference" of the artist's control a secondary thing, the painter serving as a kind of doorman to open up the gates and let the sunlight pour its scintillating golden cobwebs over the canvas or mark its sinister black shadows against the vast white surface of canvas placed on the floor and paint literally flung from a stick across the surface.

Selection plays its part, of course, no matter how accidentally the effects are achieved. There is the selection of paint, the tone and color; there is a choice of size and over-all technique—when to start—and more important—when to stop. But compared to the closely directed techniques of most traditional painting with its carefully prepared plans to help visualize the finished painting, the Abstract "action-painter" digs something out of himself and his subconscious with minimum preconception. The simple ingredient of the mix

BEACH by Charles Golden (1958). In The Brooklyn Museum Collection. Ochre sand, red and blue agitations of calligraphy in contrast to the large flat areas of sand. A finely conceived canvas from a nature motif seen afresh.

MEMORIES by Kenzo Okada. Collection of Whitney Museum of American Art, New York. A modern poetic statement. Soft warm grays and off-whites carefully patterned on the large canvas surface. Oriental themes suggested in the dark shapes and accented forms.

seems to be this—the starting on its lively way of the paint and watching it reach its inevitable conclusion, its own destiny of growing to a predestined finish.

That there is a mystic quality in this is obvious and it is not surprising that the word "Zen" enters into the discussion quite often, with all its mysteries of spirit, psychic energy, dispassionate contemplation and dependence on the abstruse and irrational. It is evident, too, that all is not clear-cut

and sure in the minds of many artists who are included in the Abstract Expressionist and Abstract Impressionist schools, the latter being a modern non-objective "Impressionism" based on nature. This they admit readily and some of their statements are as confused and entangled as their paintings. Philip Guston, one of the New York painters whose works are marked with much originality and success, stated that "painting seems like an impossibility, with only a sign now and then of its own light. Which must be because of the narrow passage from a diagraming to that other state—a corporeality." And this more lucid statement, "Usually I am on a work for a long stretch, until a moment arrives when the air of the arbitrary vanishes and the paint falls into positions that feel destined."

James Brooks says, "The painting surface has always been the rendezvous of what the painter knows with the unknown, which appears for the

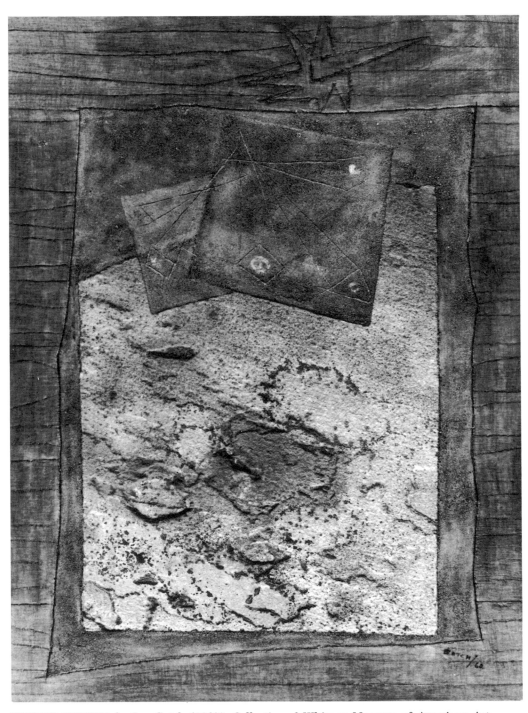

SUMMER TUNDRA by Lee Gatch (1962). Collection of Whitney Museum of American Art, New York. Gift of Mr. and Mrs. Robert M. Benjamin. A beautifully organized painting using a variety of natural textures. Natural stone and mixed media mounted on plywood.

MISTY MORNING by Gabor Peterdi. In The Brooklyn Museum Collection. A high-keyed rhythmic design with a subtle interplay of close color harmony using curved lines and lozenge shapes in sweeping movements across the canvas. Another interpretation from the objective world.

first time. An engrossment in the process of changing formal relations is the painter's method of relieving his self-consciousness as he approaches the mystery he hopes for . . ."

Duthuit, in the catalog of an exhibit of paintings by Riopelle in 1945, wrote that the work of this French-Canadian painter was ". . . a kind of aerial impressionism, extremely fickle, adapting its fury to the capacity of the executor, and ruling it in powerful rhythms. Most painters desire to be a force of nature integrated into nature, and to lose control in order to gain a certain explosive vigour, a constant source of masterpieces."

Perhaps the clue to much contemporary work is in this last statement—the painter "losing control only to gain strength" and the direct flow of his personality into his work. This "energizing" does

have much in common with the oriental painters who knew, centuries ago, how to channel the deep inner forces within themselves onto paper—the *Tao*—the ritual disposition that demanded that painting would not be a mere technical performance, no matter how skillful, but an extension of the art of living and "expression of maturity" practiced by scholars and poets and brilliant minds in the professions. It is fascinating to study the masters of Chinese calligraphy whose brushwork produced masterpieces of exquisite taste and beauty—forms and written symbols that are treasured today as works of art—abstract and energized markings that have influenced many of our contemporary painters such as Mark Tobey, Tomlin, Graves and others.

There are many ways of painting in the

spontaneous, energetic and tachist manner (using the accidental qualities in a painting). As a beginner art student, many of these freedoms may act only as snares and pitfalls often leaving the young painter bogged down in too-easy solutions or imitative repetitions of fashionable modes. For the older painter, too, who has found his way to a hard-won idiom of his own after many years, the problem can be a profound one. The constant pull between the urge to renew oneself in a fresh surge of expression or to carry on in a more traditional manner, has caught many a fine painter in the midst of his career. Whether to "stay with the figurative—or to return to it"—seems to be a question haunting many of my professional friends.

As a thinking person, you cannot but be aware of

WOMAN, II, by Willem de Kooning (1952). Collection, Museum of Modern Art, New York. Gift of Mrs. John D. Rockefeller, 3rd. De Kooning himself has said that he always seems to be wrapped in the melodrama of vulgarity. Perhaps that is the clue to understanding his series of "Women" paintings. Here the meaning of contemporary Expressionism becomes quite apparent with its forceful technique and use of distortion for emphasis.

Abstract Expressionism. The two paintings by Leonard Brooks key small touches of brilliant color to contrasting backgrounds of subdued tonalities.

all the surging seas of contemporary searching toward significant expressions in paint for our times and world. As a student, unless you *are* aware and keenly interested, there is not much point in your bothering with even the elementary pursuits of wielding the brush, for your interest will lag soon after the first simple successes.

Does the artist "see" his picture completely and fully developed in his mind before he begins to put it on canvas? Does the Abstract painter conceive his painting within himself in a finished form which has only to be projected on the canvas with suitable mechanical techniques? Generally, the answer is "no." He does have a "sensing" of what the painting will be like when it is finished, but seldom is it clearly defined and sharply etched. Mostly, the

picture grows from the first stroke to the last in an organized manner, one touch demanding another. Painting is in some ways an act of eliminating—of taking away—in that the artist sets up the problem, a line here, a spot there, making adjustments and correcting relationships as he works, eliminating and painting away the irritations of bad color, faulty composition, indecisive form, until the picture feels complete and whole. When nothing need be added or taken away, the picture is finished.

We will try this approach—the free and emotional expression of the gesture, or "action painting"—in the next section. This will be a contrast to the formal and closely disciplined exercises suggested in the "Fractured Image."

FIGURE by Jean-Denis Cruchet. A painting by a young Swiss sculptor used as a study for a three-dimensional work. The selection of strong light and dark areas to suggest form and space and the strong pattern of tones enliven the picture surface.

An Assignment in Action Painting

Today we will try our hand at a freely expressed "action" painting. To do this we will need plenty of paint (two or three tubes of oil colors will do— an umber, black, and white), a large canvas, a good space to work in and a store of energy ready to be turned loose. If *this* approach is the usual one for you—you will have served your experiment by doing the formalism assignment and will already be back at work in your usual manner. If it is not your approach, you will find it a change to roll up your sleeves, stand well back from the canvas and plunge into the fray with everything you have in the way of a determined and exciting attack on the brazen blank whiteness before you.

What will you paint? How will you paint it? What are you trying for? These are questions you will not have time to worry about this morning. The paint is squeezed out on the flat table top; the brushes, rollers, rags and spatulas are nearby and the job awaits you. If you do not have the urge to pick up a brush and start to sully and destroy the enticing surface in front of you, wait until you do. If the time is now, start! Make some marks, place a stroke here, a dot there, start the action flowing. The proportion of the canvas will suggest its own energizing if you give it a chance. The difficult part is now—the jump into the cold water. It is the same for most of us, this first plunge. Once you have made a start, using perhaps a thinned turpentine solution of paint that can easily be moved about or wiped off with a cloth if need be, you will find yourself adding and subtracting lines and masses as you are painting. Painting is, as we

have said, often a process of elimination, of correction and realignment. Perhaps this stress seems wrong, this movement destroys our design, this accent is wrongly placed. Let the mind suggest these things to you as you work; it is surprising how your instincts will reveal themselves in the matter of balance and harmony of your canvas and how they will work for you if you do not freeze up. Letting go is *not* easy, and to do so you must consciously be able to break down all the barriers of neatness, orderliness and rationality.

If you are an inexperienced painter, it will not be long before you find out that there is more to this "splashing" about than there seems to be until you have tried it for yourself. "Silly" shapes will emerge —weak, awkward and ineffectual visual entanglements that refuse to function as you wish them to. You know they do not "sit well," but why or how to correct the fault may evade you. The broad slash of confidence with which you put down the first stroke or two has become lost in a hundred bits and pieces having no relation to the original visual idea you are presenting. Counter strokes may have destroyed the first glorious simplicity that pleased you so. Unless you have been through this battle many times, as professional artists have, you will soon find out that the casual and free forms you may have often thought about in others' painting as "I like it all right, but the trouble is, it's too easy. Anybody could do that" are not as easy to obtain as you imagined. But you are learning. The first step has been taken.

YDRA by York Wilson.

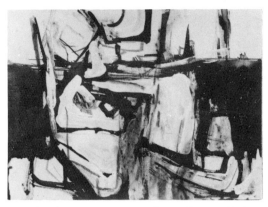

1, 2. Trial compositions in charcoal and black ink. These were developed from small sketch-book notes.

3. The first charcoal lines are drawn on the canvas using pinned-up sketches as a beginning reference.

4, 5. Using broad house-painter brushes, the first thin layers of paint are brushed in broadly. A medium of turpentine and linseed oil (in small quantity) is used for quick drying.

6. Over the thin underpainting, thick oil paint has been brushed on and palette-knife strokes applied. At this point, colored papers are often useful. Move pieces about the composition, affix them with tape to help develop the picture by trial and error, paint in the section afterwards, when you are satisfied.

7. The painting nearly completed. Smaller brushes have been used for linear calligraphy. The study is completed in one go with vigorous concentration. Note center section where a small area of collage was included.

Gouache and Ink by Staritsky (1962).

Oil on Canvas by Marcelle Ferron.

Oil on Board by Frank Avray Wilson (1962).

Collage by Leonard Brooks (1961).

Doodles

Doodles? Scribbles on a telephone pad? Anybody can do these? Try it! Below are eight "free-form" scribbles made with a bamboo stick pen as studies for small decorative spots. These are actual size and were done rapidly one after the other. Let your calligraphic sense work for you and see if you can do this, making each one varied and spirited. You will find that it is not as easy to do as it looks.

Out of the eight, one or two will seem better than others. Ask yourself "why?" The answer will be that they will contain within themselves variations, balance, repetitions, accents, dominance, and many elements affecting the design factor. Changes and additions are made as the figure grows from the first line to the last. Each mark suggests further changes—what is called "creative fluidity" becomes much in evidence—the ideas developing on the first spot or line made. A few pages of this exercise will soon prove the value of free and flowing drawing of an automatic kind.

The same principle will be valuable when you face your first large abstract painting. To prepare yourself for this, try a number of smaller panels in color, working directly without previous sketches. The four panels shown in color on page 105 were done in this manner as warming-up exercises before tackling a large painting. Crayons, casein, watercolor or oil—any of these will serve for your color exercises in the "doodle" style.

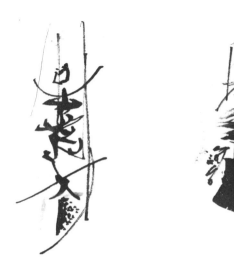

1

2

The Doodle Developed. Here are three illustrations showing how the doodle designs can be developed far beyond a first simple scrawl. Inventive and free forms can be painted in a direct and spontaneous manner once you have mastered the art of space-filling. The "relaxed control" suggested in the introduction comes into full play here. The dynamics of pictorial space, the use of texture and color, the exploiting to the full of the qualities of a media—all of these must come together to add up to a complete plastic statement.

1. A black and white oil sketch, an advanced doodle of free gesture and brush work.

2. An oil panel 8 by 10 inches using brush and knife textures in orange-reds, ochres and blacks. A lively opposition of vertical and circular movements.

3. A direct watercolor based on a musical theme. The contrast of the weighty black column and linear curved line and accent—the high notes of a violin sonata against the piano bass, perhaps.

3

STUDIO CORNER by Leonard Brooks. Oil. This painting
was done in one session, working in a manner similar to
that demonstrated on page 88. The color and form grew
from observation of a corner in the studio that were inter-
preted freely and away from the actual subject.

VERTICAL COLLAGE

Two large panels by Leonard Brooks. Both are collages of a purely nonrepresentational nature containing much decorative impact.

FROM ITALY

A BASIC ALPHABET
FOR ABSTRACT PICTURE MAKING

Some of the design means that have been and are being used by abstract painters are illustrated here. A number of design elements have been drawn to suggest a simplified alphabet for the making of abstract pictures. This list is a short one which could be extended and amplified for pages, but it will serve as a basic alphabet for the understanding of elementary principles in the language of abstraction.

Many of these illustrations overlap and the endless possiblities of new combinations are evident. Rhythm, line and mass, contrast, harmony —most compositions will *combine* a number of these design factors. Isolating a basic and theoretical element will help you understand how pictures are constructed, what makes them "work," but it is unwise to depend on these theories as infallible formulas. They are meant, as are all rules and theories in art, as helpful guides to sort out the many expressive *means*, the plastic images the modern artist has found helpful in expressing his personal world.

Today in most exhibitions, you will find evidence of these manipulations of line, mass and space in contemporary pictures, for never in the history of art has the artist stripped away so much superfluous matter to reach the core of his creativity nor has he presented his creations so starkly and so uncompromisingly shorn of pleasing seductive trimmings. In this age of specialization in all fields and professions, we will find artists applying themselves to the research and study of one facet of their profession with the tenacity and fervor of a scientist. One man will find the square a source of infinite expression— Josef Albers has devoted a lifetime to the colored square—another will pursue the subtle tonal harmony to its final conclusion, a black on black or a white on white; others, leaving all such intellectual pursuits, will grasp the emotionally charged paint brush to fill their canvas with the fiery churnings of their painterly convictions.

Analyses such as those shown here may help you discover and know the many non-figurative idioms and stylizations, which have become as much accepted in the contemporary world of art as the more traditional methods that once shocked the art world, such as Impressionist "broken" touches of pigment or Fauve flamboyancy.

As you study more, you will discover that the variety of non-figurative techniques is as varied, if not more so, as the more traditional ways of painting. Many of the design elements used are our old friends from academic days re-adapted from the world of figurative painting to the needs of abstraction. A careful search of our art history books reveals that nothing is really new; an eleventh-century Spanish fresco, richly preserved in all its glowing color reminds us that men long ago knew how to deliver their message with force on flat walls by the use of simplified color schemes, distortions, powerful designs and compositions far removed from the weak and derivative "realism" of later centuries. It was not by accident that Picasso and Derain collected African primitive art and used the lessons learned from studying it to their own advantage, long before it became fashionable to accept such grotesqueries as fine art. Today, the artist and poet follow with wonder the endless new forms and worlds presented to them by our new space age, by the revolutionary concepts of nature and its meaning, and by our rapidly unfolding era of scientific marvels and man's relation to them. Here indeed, is new material for the artist's brush and pen, new moods, new sensations, new feelings.

This simplified basic alphabet will serve to build a vocabulary needed to understand the language of abstract painting. These drawings illustrate a number of ways of designing abstract motifs, using a few of the many elements of visual sensation.

Many of these design principles are well-worn and accepted to the point of becoming clichés if not used in a sensitive and subtle manner. Nevertheless, they contain some of the basic expressive counterpoints that you will probably use, alone or combined, to make your abstract pictures alive and vital without dependence on allusive or representational subject matter. Within the black-and-white limitation of the illustrations shown, they will suggest a few of the many ways awaiting you for experiment. A number of color reproductions (pages 61 and 105) suggest further exercises for study.

1. The fractured image concept. Semi-figuration based on subject matter and transposed to form lively patterns of light and dark, lost and found areas on the picture plane. An idiom used by Braque and others of the Cubist tradition and recently brought to its full development by the late Jacques Villon, whose work is a *must* for study of contemporary modified Cubism.

2. The impact of large simple forms placed within the picture plane with little relation to the edges. Careful modulation of contour and silhouetted edges by cutting into the dark passages. In the tradition of Chinese calligraphy with mystic and symbolic overtones. Looks much easier to do than it actually is. Try it.

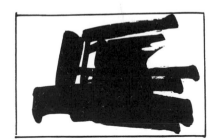

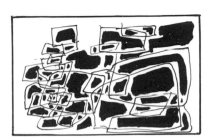

3. Line and mass. Contrasting lines combined with heavy blacks spotted with care for variety of size and shape. Reminiscent of pebbles on the beach, or stone walls. Such textured areas provide pleasurable visual sensations in black and white or color.

4. Contrast of shape and tone. The white circle emphasized and made important by surrounding black areas. A balanced opposition of light and dark; one of the many ways interest is given to the picture. A device skillfully used by traditional artists to give liveliness to the composition.

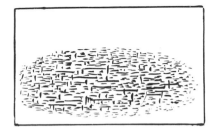

5. Dots, dashes, repetitions of all-over patterns have a fascination for some painters. You will find many examples of this manner, sometimes rich in tone and color. The Middleton painting (page 128) is a good example of this interest in all-over agitation of the picture surface.

6. The use of light patches on dark. A semi-formalist mode much admired by certain French painters—Mannesier, Bissière, Bazaine, Esteve. Semi-formalist, carefully painted and planned, it used no accidental qualities to provide its surface with attractive qualities.

7. Large, open forms using a secondary tone in addition to black and white. Edges are carefully shaped, not nearly so accidental as it may appear. The American painter Kline loved the large black-and-white gesture.

8. Constructivist and formal. Lines and areas geometrically conceived. Flat surface of picture plane preserved with depth and space cancelled out in an uncompromising and calculated breaking up of the picture area. Sometimes such work does not go much beyond the decorative.

9. Accidental spottings and drippings of ink form the activating agent here. Blots and scrawls enliven the surface. Try making such patterns without touching the paper. Combine such textures with careful overdrawing.

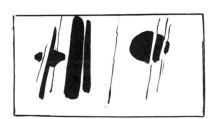

10. Irradiation of the white surface with carefully chosen lines and spots placed with careful regard to the pull and influence of the side and top confining lines of the picture plane. Suggestive of natural forms; an oriental concept saying much with little.

11. Symbols and images of a personal notation dug up from the subconscious; inventions of forms and colors and shapes fused to a high sophisticated expression. Miró is one of the greatest exponents of such paintings using amorphic shapes. Also see Jean Arp, Masson and others.

12. Lively movement created by the use of rhythmic linear pattern. The filling of space with such free patterns can also be studied and contrasted by the use of more formal shapes such as the square, circle and pyramid.

Socrates said:

> I will try to speak of the beauty of shapes, and I do
> not mean the shapes of living figures, or their
> imitations in painting, but I mean straight lines
> and curves and the shapes made by them, by the
> lathe, ruler or square. They are not beautiful for
> any particular reason or purpose, as other things
> are, but are eternally and by their nature, beautiful,
> and give pleasure of their own quite free from the
> itch of desire; and in this way colors can give
> similar pleasures. . .

Such early musings on Non-Objective and geometric types of paintings may well fascinate us. All of us know how difficult it is to discuss with originality and lucidity the many problems of pictorial composition. If it could be done with finality, there would be no need of painting at all. Words would do it for us. Nevertheless, there are points we can mull over and think about and elucidate; hints and suggestions drawn from the experience of actual *doing* which will help us. How involved musings alone can become will be seen in some of the critical publications of the international art world. Even the *Pedagogical Sketchbook of Paul Klee* will seem simple compared to these effusions, though it tackles such problems as "Kinetic and Chromatic Energy," analyzes two dimensionality in terms of gravity, symbols of form in motion, and more, illustrated with charts and drawings as strange as Klee's paintings themselves. This little volume, the first part a planned course for Bauhaus students, should be read by all art students. What could be more explicit and yet beguiling than this statement from the book, "An *active* line on a walk, moving freely, without goal. A walk for a walk's sake. The mobility agent is a point, shifting its position forward."

Studies Developed from the Alphabet

Here and on the next pages are a number of studies in various media. Each one is related to the abstract alphabet illustrated previously. If you have read the captions you can easily sort out the many different styles and combinations of stylizations. Some are more formalized than others, some are of an automatic kind; calligraphy, accidental spottings and textures, controlled edges, spatial overlappings, all of these can be noted. The subjects range from semi-abstract figuration to complete non-objective forms. All were painted in a series of experimental sessions similar to those outlined for self-study in "A Year's Course" on pages 136, 137.

These illustrations may suggest to you the myriad ways in which the basic alphabet can be used. The one rule that may help you in doing these exercises is this, *do not try and say too many things in the one picture*. Remember the basic point you are exploring and stick to it, even at risk of having it become obvious. This is much better than losing all consistency and ending up with utter confusion of aim and direction.

1. An attempt to hold the energy of many movements in a free overall writing of light and dark. A derivation of a "cityscape."

2. A more formalized pastel in which the edges and well-defined light note are played against semi-geometric forms.

3. Large open shapes form a background for the textures of fibered paper set in the center of this composition. A collage using torn edges for variety.

4. A casein freely conceived. The stress of large vertical movement is counteracted by the horizontal and diagonal background strokes.

101

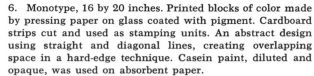

6. Monotype, 16 by 20 inches. Printed blocks of color made by pressing paper on glass coated with pigment. Cardboard strips cut and used as stamping units. An abstract design using straight and diagonal lines, creating overlapping space in a hard-edge technique. Casein paint, diluted and opaque, was used on absorbent paper.

5. An orange and green panel derived from recollections of Luxembourg Gardens, Paris. Rich impastos and scumbling of oil paint strokes are employed to give color variation of pigment.

7. A freely brushed oil with strong contrasts. Accidental runs and dripped paint controlled and formed to give variety to brush work and textures. The colors are rich, golden hues and yellows. A spontaneous action painting, 16 by 20 inches.

Jan de Swart, an outstanding artist-designer of California, has created many fine murals. He says of his 120 foot mural, pictured below—an aluminum casting made in conjunction with wood moulds:

It requires the will to create, the willingness to let creation take place . . . It is a process toward the organic, influenced by innumerable organizing forces that shape whatever is complete and balanced . . . where the ugly and beautiful are one; where there is order in devastation; where the accidental is most directed, the most adjusted; where there is no tension but all-tension; where meaning springs from the merging of opposites.

This mural is one of the many new and wonderful works this contemporary sculptor has done. His words describing the creative process that he feels brings about the final result he wishes are very applicable to contemporary painting. The "forces" set in motion, paint against paint; the "accidents" of pigment and medium and brushwork directed and controlled while the growing process takes place, the organic interlocking of all the elements of the painting into a completeness and balance which seem inevitable, a "rightness" that could be no other way.

The illustration above is a contemporary mural by Jan de Swart which uses the light and dark qualities of many varied textures and modellings of space in the modern manner. Nonfigurative, it emanates its own "subject" having much in common with painterly concepts of the abstract artist today.

Color Exercises from the Alphabet

When you are in an experimental mood try a number of color exercises based on the abstract alphabet drawings suggested on pages 97 and 98. Using varied media and techniques, choose several approaches to increase your inventive capacities in design making. Casein or gouache will be found valuable in making small but complete paintings (8 by 10 inches) or pastel and crayon will help with suggestive free-form strokes and markings. Choose the best from these small sketches and use them as the basis for larger fully worked oil paintings. Such studies will increase your understanding of the works of other painters as well as expanding your own creative capacities.

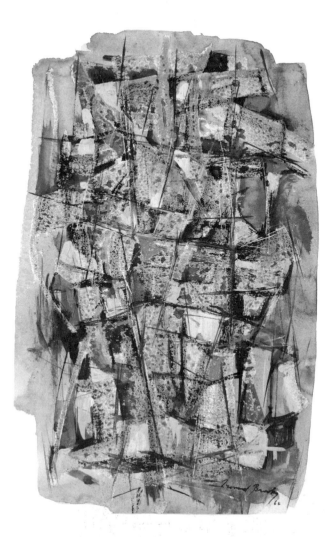

Experimental Color Panels

Watercolor, crayon and casein are combined in these experimental color panels, opposite, based on the Abstract Alphabet shown on previous pages. Drawing, color and technique combine in a statement that has grown from the first stroke to the last in an organic pattern demanding its own conclusion.

This untidy corner of the studio holds assorted papers, cloths, pieces of netting, tissues, old posters, and faded papers peeled from old walls. Large sheets of prepared casein, colored papers in brilliant hues or soft tones of grays, browns and blacks are made in advance for a permanent color palette of papers. Such a scrap box is a happy hunting ground for odds and ends of color and texture. Don't make it too neat or file away such materials in too organized a fashion—part of the collage technique issues from the very surprises lurking in the untidy clutter. Save the neatness for other enterprises than collage!

MODERN TECHNIQUES AND METHODS

Paper and Rags—The Collage

In 1450, the Venetian painter Crivelli was enriching his paintings with thick gesso overlays, imbedding and gluing real jewels into the rich golden background of outlined high relief. In the sixteenth century, butterflies were used by the Aztecs in sumptuous patterns of iridescence. Inlays, glued-on fabrics and barks are found in many primitive decorations and fetishes. All of this took place long before 1912 when Picasso decided to stick a piece of printed material imitating the caning of a chair onto one of his pictures, thus inventing the contemporary art of papier collé, or what became later known as "Collage."

This, along with the first works of Braque, was the first use of collage as a serious art form. These collages, made from wallpaper, colored and printed papers, cigarette packages, bus tickets, were generally small decorative experiments, often conceived as studies for larger pictures or as an ephemeral bit of research which was not taken too seriously or profoundly as a work of art. Many of these, although crumbling and fading, are carefully preserved in museums and galleries as manifestations of one part of a master's work and research.

GUITAR AND WINE GLASS by Picasso. McNay Art Institute, San Antonio, Texas. An early collage combining wallpapers, music, drawing and cut papers. One of the infinite styles and experiments of the most original and creative artist of our times.

106

MERZ: SANTA CLAUS (Der Weihnachtsmann) by Kurt Schwitters (1922). Collection, The Museum of Modern Art, New York. A pioneer in collage, Cubist influenced, uses papers, cloths, tickets, and so on. A Dadaist, Schwitters was a master experimenter in the use of textures.

Nearly all the first collages were small, semi-abstractions derived from subject matter such as violins, guitars, wine bottles, and so on, put through the fracturing and distorting mill of the cubists' mind and eye.

A second grouping that contributed to collage history is made up from the work of the Dadaists— Ernst, Breton, Tanguy, Schwitters. This group came on the scene in 1918 with strange and fantastic paintings and collages of dream worlds and wondrous images dredged from the subconscious. Less concerned with the plastic and aesthetic values of collage, they put together pictures of the irrational, using incongruous elements in a fresh and sometimes shocking manner. Photo-montage (reassembled bits of photographs) or combinations of photographs and drawings or paintings became a strong part of the Dadaists' and Surrealists' vocabulary. The nightmare qualities of Hieronymus Bosch's fifteenth-century Gothic world took on new Freudian significance when the Surrealists began to use a similar detailed technique with the addition of contemporary subject matter—telephones, motorcars, machines.

The eye-catching and thought-provoking content of these new twentieth century paintings caused much consternation in the world of the academic and conservative painter. But it was not long before new sensations appeared and the Surrealists' works became absorbed and adapted to the modern world. Posters and commercial advertising took

STILL LIFE by Alfredo Zalce. Here this well-known Mexican painter uses large, simple areas in yellow, browns, green and violet to compose a cut-paper collage. An example of how the flat shapes of straight cut-out silhouette forms can be arranged in a decorative pattern. Textures are eliminated and a poster-like effect is intended.

TANGIER by William Harris. An amusing and skillful use of textural qualities. The oriental motif has been put together with curtain lace, colored and striped fabrics, bamboo strips, and canvas of various weaves. Not an abstraction but a clear demonstration of visual interest given to the surface of the picture by using assorted textures of actual materials.

Collage by Beatrice Mandelman. Scissor and razor-cut shapes of bright hue suggestive of growth and plant forms. Cut and assembled in a number of overlapping areas making a lively collage.

over the techniques and used them to their purposes. During the twenties "arte moderne" became the fashion, infecting furniture and industrial products with pseudo-cubist designs, floor lamps of circles and squares, bedrooms in red and black straight lines; posters became imitative of Cubist fracturing of planes; advertising used the photo-montage for illustration. The "jazz age" period had set in earlier and art, like music, tried to express itself in new ways using the new forms of the twentieth century as legitimate material. Who of that generation can ever forget the riot of angles, circles, diagonal shapes suddenly appearing on murals, buildings and every kind of object that wanted to look smart and up-to-date? Today, many of these stylizations look curiously old-fashioned. What we have to put in their place, we will consider in another part of the book. What is of interest to us here is how much the collage contributed in these early years to the simplification of design and the break away from realism toward the use of the abstract idiom.

Many of us can recall our kindergarten days when we proudly brought home our first cut-out paper "art work." A Halloween pumpkin, a round red apple with a clean green leaf—flat one-color silhouette shapes scissored out of cheap construction paper and pasted down on another colored page. Perhaps these days, youngsters are weaned away from such unsophisticated "realism." I hope not, for if they are they will miss a lot of fun.

Why are we concerned with investigating the collage—a more advanced form of assembling papers and materials than we knew in our school days? It is true that lately there has been a vigorous interest in this medium and that the showing of collages in important exhibitions has become quite routine. To appreciate the particular qualities of the collage we should know something of its history and techniques, just as we must study the watercolor or oil mediums in order to understand them.

The justification for seriously studying collage methods here is that it will help you understand some of the complex problems of abstraction. The collage is an ideal way of approaching many of the major considerations to be faced in working in the abstract idiom.

There is release of imagination for the student when the interposing craft of cutting or tearing shapes of paper removes him from "copying" too literally from nature with a brush or pencil. The suggestive qualities brought about by the accidental conjunction of varied materials in the scrap-box, the textures and combinations of colors spread in front of the collage-maker before he selects and assembles them, open up ideas and worlds of visual interest that cannot be conjured up quite as readily when confronted with the squeezed-out pigment on the standard palette or watercolor box. The pictorial composition is more likely to start itself.

Another practical factor that makes the acquiring of collage skill worth while is its usefulness as a trial and error method. Unlike paint, the shapes and colors can be shuffled about on the picture, arranged in many ways, altered and

1

2

modified *before* fixing the separate parts permanently. Many professional painters use this system of trial as an auxiliary to their traditional techniques of painting and drawing. Often a difficult problem of where an accent should go, or a change of a colored area, can be solved by sticking paper or other material on the painting temporarily with adhesive tape or a pin before correcting in pigment. Step back from the picture and imagine the texture or color as part of the completed picture.

Recently, while studying Chagall's first sketches for his series of stained glass windows for Jerusalem, it could be seen how his small conceptual pages for the first visualization used collage areas of bright patches of colored papers to help design the finished windows. Line drawings over these suggested the leading lines. It is revealing to see the final result—the light pouring through an area of glowing yellow glass, conceived in the beginning of his work as a pasted-down, cut-out piece of tinted paper.

Collage Demonstration

Illustration 1, opposite, shows a large collage mural in process of development. Three large Masonite board panels, mounted on wooden stretchers and braced to prevent warping, are assembled as one large panel and placed on a large, specially designed easel. Sections of the collage are built up with papers, glued down with white plastic glue. Medium-sized, bristle, housepainters' brushes are used for pasting, applying the glue in a mixture

diluted with water to the consistency of thin cream. A coating of this is brushed over the complete painting when finished, which seals it safely behind a transparent and washable film. The three panels can be taken apart in sections, cutting the papers with a razor blade; when reassembled, the parts can be locked together at the back with metal cross-pieces and screws.

"Appian Way," illustration 2, a large collage mural 8 feet long, 3 feet 4 inches high, is a decorative mural in off whites, blacks and muted tones of tawny browns accented with orange tones. This project was based on the ancient marbled forms and ruins of the Roman suburbs. Many kinds of Japanese papers were used to give varied transparent depths. Textures of cloth, inked and dyed papers with cut-out forms were assembled on strong reinforced stretchers, which can be separated into three sections for transporting as demonstrated in Illustration 1. Sealed behind a spraying of clear plastic, there is no reason why such an assembly should not last as long, or longer, than a traditional oil painting.

Techniques for Experiment in Collage

Listed here are a variety of technical devices and some suggestions which will be found useful in making collages. You will no doubt add to these techniques or discard many of the procedures after you have done a number of experiments to find out your personal preference and method of working.

See to it that you gather about you from time to

time bits of colored papers, cloth, scraps, and odds and ends that may be useful for collage making, as suggested in the caption under the Collage Box illustration on page 106. Some day when you feel at loose ends and painting isn't going well, take a look in your "collage box." Many a picture has come to life from the chance viewing of an appealing color harmony or conjunction of textures thrown together by accident. The sight of an old steamer ticket or letter can set off nostalgic memories, a twist of scarlet thread against a rich black may suddenly seem meaningful and in need of being put down in permanent form, snatched from oblivion by selection. In this way a picture may be started, for all is grist to the artist's mill when the creative imagination begins its work. Not for nothing will you find old stones, driftwood, dried weeds and odd pieces of stained bric-a-brac in many artists' studios. I have a small shell collection that has generated for me many a color harmony of soft whites, pinks, and delicate grays.

Collage by Leonard Brooks. Light and dark textures used to form a dramatic composition.

Collage by Leonard Brooks. Actual netting, sand and many textures form a beach motif.

FROM A SHORE, PACIFIC by Leonard Brooks. A semi-abstract subject made from memory, suggesting the staccato play of light against dark, the geometry of door and window, walled hillsides, textured shore and warm tiled roof. Subjects of this kind can still provide inspiration for the artist who will use such things as the raw material with which to begin his painting. Gray background papers, cloth strips, thread fibers, and marble dust were used here, then sealed durably and safely on a masonite panel coated with a final brushing of plastic transparent glue which acts like a varnish.

PIAZZA, by Leonard Brooks. Made from memories of similar places—the patterns of antique houses, streets, pigeons in a square. The material used was collage only, dyed cloths and papers, cut and torn papers, on a 30 by 36 inch canvas. Notice the flattening of planes and dismissal of deep space and perspective rendering in the design. These illustrations may suggest a like exercise.

An assemblage of papers and cloths in blue, black and off whites that exploits to the full the collage feeling, which is sufficient unto itself if the collage is successful. An intricate fusing of texture and abstract counterpoint.

Torn Papers

Yes, there is even an "art" to tearing up a piece of paper. A few trials will soon show you how different kinds of papers tear, some with a ragged variety of edge, others with clean sharp contours or with filaments and fibers left to form a soft and fuzzy edge when pasted down. *Quick* tearing and *slow* tearing produce different results. Knowing how to produce the kind of edge you need is as important as how to paint required edges with a brush.

Cut Papers

Use razor blade or scissors, the standard way of cutting out shapes, the paper-doll technique. Even this can reach a refined state as we saw when Matisse, confined to his sick-bed, cut direct, large, decorative shapes for wall murals or illustrations for his famed circus book. The free swing of a sharp razor blade can produce forms and lines that have all the finesse of a skillful pen or brush. Direct cutting without following a traced or drawn line will give a livelier result than a too slavish cutting out of silhouette shapes.

Torn and Cut Cloths

Experiment is needed here to find out what happens with different materials. Scraps of torn or cut cloth can be put down in jig-saw fashion, mounted in layers over each other, or used in combination with other materials, papers and so forth. Study the large pictures of the Italian painter Burri if you would see a masterful use of cloth, sacking, other materials and paint combined. The collages of Marca-Relli made from canvas and leather pieces are also of interest here.

SPANISH SHORE by Leonard Brooks

Japanese papers and cloths are combined for rich, textural qualities, transparent and opaque. "Spanish Shore" uses heavily textured underpainting with glazes over the impasto.

TUSCANY by Leonard Brooks

A collage base of stained and colored papers serves as a background on which drawn and printed lines are made. This technique may be seen in developed form in many of the collage illustrations in this book.

A Venetian theme using newsprint, colored cloths and overdrawing in black and white chalk, sprayed with fixatif when the collage was finished.

Transparent Papers

Most valuable. Collect fine papers as you would fine pigments. Japanese and Chinese rice papers of all textures and weights; tissues, thin bond, tracing paper, and the like. You will be surprised at the number of "white" papers there are—blue white, cream white, dull white, brilliant and glaring white—a hundred whites from which to select. Set down against color or gray, the choice can be a very subtle one. Use these transparent layers *over* color, to modify a black, to give depth and space to dull areas. Combine several layers over each other. Stain and mark papers before using them. The use of white papers is exciting and endless.

An effective collage made from 23 pieces of torn paper suggests the pueblo country of New Mexico. Such simple exercises make excellent use of the imagination in space filling and composing.

RED HEAD by Frank Avray Wilson. Collection, British Council, Tunis. English painter and writer Wilson has found his expression in the Abstract Expressionist style. He brings the forceful free sweep of the pigment to large canvases glowing with life and color. A believer in "Vitalism," Wilson shows striking energy and strength in his work.

AEGEAN #V by Louis Ribak. A large canvas developed from many casein studies made in Greece. Louis Ribak, well-known American painter and draftsman, has evolved the simplicity and directness of his work from years of experience with the traditional techniques of drawing and painting.

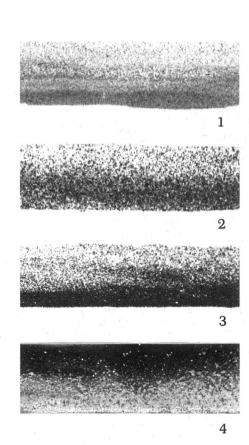

1. A fine sifted brown sand. 2. Coarse multicolored beach sand. 3. Black fine Pacific coast volcanic sand. 4. Fine textured marble dust. 5. Coarse marble dust.

Sand texture. Interesting textures may be created for collages by using various colored sands. Make sure these are not dusts that will disintegrate or crumble with time. Use only hard gravel dusts or inert materials. Sprinkled on wet plastic glue, they will hold permanently and safely. Use a piece of cardboard for a stencil where you wish to make a straight edge. Sand is often used to soften an edge of plane against plane, to enliven a dull area, or to modify an insistent passage that is too light or too dark. Experiment with the many shades and hues of brown and black sands. The illustration shows textures made with beach sands and white marble dusts.

Texture

Here of course is the true world of the collage. The limit of what you will use is only for you to decide, but don't convince yourself that if you use some material that has never been used before, you have made a masterpiece as a result. Novelty is fine, but much of it can be discounted today when we have been overdosed with it to the point where a great deal of its impact has been lost and the charm of genuine surprise dulled.

Some of the materials you may find useful for collage are new—plastic sheeting, foils and tinsels, pressed veneers and so on. Most of the standard materials employed are the same as those used by the first practitioners of the art—corrugated cardboard, canvas scraps, newspaper and magazine pages, netting, lace, natural sands in all kinds of granulations and tints, ground up marble dust, silicates. The list on page 120 suggests more materials.

Texture-making has many dangers. Permanence is more certain with the use of the new plastic glues and adhesives but even so some materials can soon grow brittle, cracking and falling apart in a short time. Fading is a real danger and it is necessary to see that papers and cloths, especially brilliantly colored materials, are subjected to bleaching and sunlight *before* being used. Cheap dyes and ordinary printing inks can change color in a few weeks if left in a strong light.

Beginners using collage textures for the first time have the inclination to gather too many contrasting assortments of materials into one grouping. Be careful to not overdo it; save something for another picture. A few well-placed highly textured areas set against large simple areas of space will often be found more effective than having every inch textured and eye-catching.

Painted and Drawn Textures

Papers and cloths stained, painted, drawn or marked with rollers or inks and paint, before using, supply plenty of variety in color or black and white patterns. Use discarded sketches and paintings on paper or canvas. Some painters prepare sheets of

Simple constructions will help your imagination and compositional abilities. Try a geometric or formal panel using pieces of wood, black stripping and objects. The aim here is to arrange a well-knit composition which satisfies your eye.

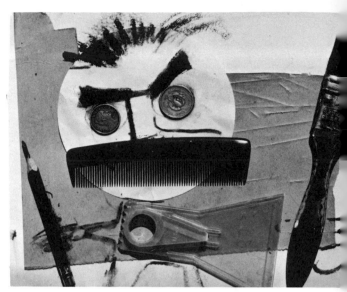

Self Portrait. An amusing exercise. Try doing a self portrait using whatever happens to be on hand. A fine way to free yourself from photographic seeing. Advertising art has taken over this technique of assemblage.

colored papers well beforehand, coating them with casein or transparent watercolor. These papers provide the bright spots of color or background for collages. They are as permanent as any painting can be and the dangers of fading are dismissed.

If you are a purist in collages you will have none of this technique, feeling that it is a form of cheating; the collage must be all assembled and depend on its torn and cut-out shapes alone; to touch it up after is "not playing the game." But most collage makers today mix all combinations of techniques, painting becomes part collage, collage becomes part painting. Anything goes if the result justifies it.

Assemblages

The use of objects in the three-dimensional world to form a composition has become quite popular. Boxes of stones, sculpture-like gluings of scrap pieces of wood, even squashed automobiles are a form of "found art." We are beyond the realm of the collage here, but recently the Museum of Modern Art, New York, put out a publication called *Assemblages* (which gives a detailed account of the collage as a creative activity) and here the "assemblage" is considered part of the evolution of collage.

Materials for Making Collages

Here is a partial list of materials you may use to make collages. The list could go on indefinitely. Part of the pleasure of collage making comes from the discovery of new and unexpected sources that can be combined in an effective manner. The limitations are yours and depend on a sense of fitness for what you wish to say.

Transparent papers	Lace
Wool and cotton threads	Embroidery
	Canvas scraps

120

Collage by Leonard Brooks. Inspired by material found in the collage box.

Old engravings
Tapestries
Grasses and other dried
    materials
Photographs
Printed material
Marble dust
Sand
Leather
Tin foil
Ropes, cord, twine
Netting

Corrugated board
Tapes, plastic and
    paper
Kleenex
Fibers
Veneered wood
Wallpaper
Posters
Wire netting
Plastic and rubber
    sheeting
Plexiglass

Mounting and Supports

Thick paper or cardboard will provide a support
on which to glue such material, though this will
often curl and warp unless it is to be set under
glass. For a base on which to glue heavy material,
such as cloth and netting, I prefer to use a
well-braced wooden frame that has masonite glued
to it. This insures that the collage will stay flat and
secure and glazing is not needed as the collage can
be exhibited like an oil painting. For large collages
a strong support is essential. The collage mural
shown on page 110 was mounted on three framed

sections strapped and bolted together and it hangs
on the wall flat and unwarped in spite of the
endless layers of glue and material applied to it.
Many collages done in Europe on a recent trip were
brought back on paper supports and mounted for
permanence at a later date.

Glues

Library paste, mucilage, rabbit skin glue, all of
these adhesives can be used to stick paper down,
but a more useful practical glue is the white
plastic glue sold under different trade names,
Elmer's, Wilhold, Resistol and others. It is a milky
white opaque liquid that dries transparently and
its great holding and binding qualities make it
invaluable for the collage maker who uses sands,
cloths, wood strips or heavier materials. It can be
diluted with water and is much easier to work with
than the traditional sticky glues. It dries rapidly
and a thin coating over the collage will seal it
under a water-proof seal when the picture is
finished. It has the advantage of rinsing out easily
from brushes—keep a jar of water at hand and do
this constantly if you want to preserve your
brushes. It keeps well in a covered jar or squeeze
container and does not change the color of the

paper or material of the collage. Do not use it to glue material onto oil ground canvas as it will not adhere safely.

Epoxy—two plastic liquids combined, which makes the strongest binder known—can be used if you wish to glue together heavy materials such as assemblages containing your old typewriter or the kitchen sink, but these are hardly necessary for the ordinary collage.

With these simple things—papers, souvenir scraps and odds and ends, plus glue and a support on which to stick things down—you are ready to begin your first collage.

A First Experiment

To get yourself in trim, the way a violinist runs his fingers up and down the scale before beginning to play, spend a few minutes testing your materials. Take a few pieces of paper and tear up a number of free shapes (Figure 1). Place them at random on a sheet of old paper and move them about. When you feel you have made some kind of arrangement that appeals to you, stick them down. If you are using white plastic glue you need not worry about the edges of the glue showing on the paper as the glue marks will dry transparently and not show in the final version. Coat the paper with a diluted glue mixed up beforehand. Add more water and see how liquid it can become and still dry tightly, adhering to the paper. Try a coating *over* the paper and watch it dry. Test a piece of cloth, soak it well *through* the cloth or dip it in a jar of glue, smooth it out and see what happens when dry. Does it bubble up, does it lie flat? Try a scrap of transparent paper over a colored background paper. Try a piece of tissue, a scrap of cardboard. All very obvious and simple steps but each one should become so familiar that you need not think about any of them when you are really in the full excitement of making a collage. Try a thicker coating of glue on masonite; sprinkle marble dust or fine sand on it, tap the masonite to drop off superfluous particles and see if the sand dries immovable from the board.

1 2

Try tearing the paper *away* from the collage while it is still semi-wet (Figure 2). Fold an edge of tissue over into the wet glue making a hard sharp edge. Paste overlays of paper and cloth on other layers.

All these ways are part of an easy craft but it is surprising how much can be done with them when directed and foreseen by an experienced hand.

Now you are ready for a more complex step. Use some black paper scraps, a page of newsprint, a tone or two of buff paper. Arrange these into some kind of order, spacing them to give interest, intervals varied, an accent selected and placed where it seems to suit your eye. Find a *very* white white paper. Spot it out as a contrast to the black areas. Keep away from making houses or animals or images. This is your exercise in pure abstraction, to make those bits and pieces interesting without visual imitations of forms or symbols or reference to *things*. If a snake or a house does emerge, obliterate it. This is a conscious effort to be non-objective. (Figure 3.)

A few minutes juggling and shuffling and you should be ready to glue down the page or half-page

3

4

5

collage. Let it dry, a matter of half an hour or so. Draw over it with charcoal, adding smudges or lines where you seem to feel they "tie" the areas together, but keep these marks to a minimum.

Your next exercise can be done while the previous one is drying. Use the same materials and colors. Add scraps of canvas or cloth. The illustration here (Figure 4) uses the primed and unprimed sides of left-over canvas. Fine black sand was added while the collage was still wet. The sharp line was made by holding an edge of cardboard over the glue and using it as a stencil guard while the sand was dropped into the wet

glue. Two black papers gave different blacks and edges. One torn paper gave soft edges, the other clean edges. Here again we have an Abstraction, though if we wish we could easily see subject matter in this one—how about "Winter Fields" for example? Turn it into a vertical and it becomes more abstract.

Figure 5 is a seven-inch collage making mountain forms and a lake from some black and white bits plus newsprint and torn whites in two tones.

In these five small collages we have learned the main basic techniques for collage making.

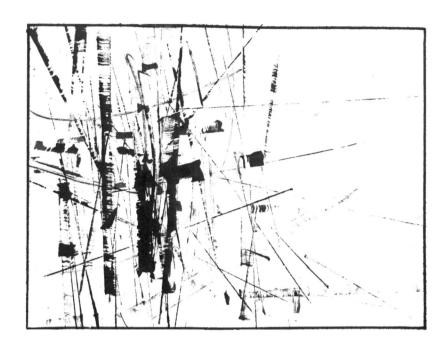

Textural Devices

Following on your experiments with collage and as a spur to the imagination, the use of unorthodox and untried media is suggested. Setting aside brushes and pens and pencils for these new tools for a morning's work will often provide a stimulus when inspiration lags.

A bottle of black or blue ink, a few strips of cardboard and some sheets of scrap paper for experiment and you are ready for work. Further textural devices can be added to this simple technique and you will perhaps add variations of your own. Try oil or casein paint instead of inks, or other forms of making lines and shapes in this technique which is essentially a way of *printing* marks and has innumerable variations.

The use of such material will free you from too much concern over using the brush or pen in a timid manner; you must make up your mind and put a strong line or stroke down. It will help you also to think in abstract pattern-making. Limit yourself to the straight and diagonal line, rejecting all curved lines. Structure and repetition of horizontal and vertical lines will provide you with strong picture-making essentials. Plan out a composition if you wish, but it will be better for these first experimental efforts to just "let go" and allow the paper to be filled with trial lines in various directions overprinted until you feel satisfied with the divisions of space and repetitions of suggested planes.

Use strips of scrap cardboard and dip the edge in ink or paint spread out on a tray or flat surface. Using this cardboard as a printing form, press the edge on paper. Try dragging it sideways or ruffle the edge of the card for an irregular edge that prints a "broken" line.

An ordinary pipe cleaner—the wire covered, bristle kind—dipped into ink and used as a pen can produce sharp edges, dragged edges, spatter effects . . . all without use of other tools. Try this over roller surfaces along with the cardboard edge technique. See "New Tools," page 134.

The next section demonstrates further techniques that will enliven the experimental mood and add new means to your expressive purposes. Artists have always known the value of exploiting the peculiar qualities of individual media and their characteristics. These techniques, studied along with the new materials suggested in "Materials" on page 134 may help you find a way of working most suitable to yourself.

"New means, new subjects." Braque, 1917.

"I believe that any art of suggestion gets much from the reaction of the surface of the medium itself upon the artist. A truly sensitive artist does not find the same image in two different media, because they strike him differently." Redon, 1898.

THE FORUM, ROME. Studies made on the spot. Wash, and pen-and-ink were used to note down architectural facts and composition. The drawings were developed at a later date into two large abstract paintings, shown on the facing page. Much of the detail was put aside and only the large forms kept. These, with memories of color and mood brought the final canvas into being. Another example of the value of sketches to help develop a finished work.

Sketch Book Studies

In making a synthesis from natural forms, there are a number of steps the artist must consider. The making of sketches and analytical notes will often help him in the transfiguration from the facts before him. The chances are, even if he is a trained painter and accustomed to seeing with the "painter's eye," he will want to jot down a note or make a sketch of what he intends to do in paint before beginning a large canvas. This was truer of the Cubist technique than it is of the more spontaneous type of "action painting" which we discussed before.

The ability to "see" the essential forms and underlying structure of objects, figures and landscapes comes only with training. Ben Shahn has said, "*Intuition* in art is actually the result of prolonged *tuition*. The so-called 'innocent eye' does not exist."

Sketching and selective noting of facts is a relative thing. How many times will the artist be surprised while sketching by the comments of onlookers who make such statements as, "I wonder where he sees *that* color?" or "I don't know where he gets *that* line from, he certainly sees differently than I do." And this even if the artist happens to be a super-realistic renderer in watercolor. How varied and differently we each see and take what appeals to us from the cold facts. I have sketched with many artist friends over the years and long ago have learned not to be surprised at the different individual interpretations they make in front of nature.

Many painters whose final works are "non-objective" and seem to contain nothing of figurative matter often spend time sketching and drawing from nature. Recently, I spent a month in Venice with a well-known abstract painter who devoted every day to making color panels and notes from the actual scene. In this way, he felt he could absorb the new sensations and feelings and eventually filter them through the fine screen of his personality into the large and vigorous canvases that he paints.

This intake of visual sensation is a mysterious

quality that most professional painters know how to exploit. Soaking up color and form is essential; without it the wells of creativity soon run dry and it is not without reason that most painters like to shake themselves out of a too well-known environment from time to time, to subject themselves to new and strange surroundings. Here the sketch book studies can be invaluable.

Some abstract painters reject this "beginning with nature" premise and state that they prefer to have no direct relation with nature and objective forms as we know them. Later, they dig out of themselves a new kind of reality with personal shapes and forms bearing no relation to the objective world. If nature does slip in, or we find some context that seems to indicate a close contact with skies, water or the natural elements, it is purely accidental and as far as the painter is

THE SEINE by Leonard Brooks. Oil.

Gouache by Derek Middleton.

concerned it would be better if we did not read such things into his pictures. They would like us to read them purely as pictures, sensations of a visual kind that cannot be provoked by any other medium.

Generally, though this is not always true, a painter who has served an apprenticeship working in a figurative manner is able to swing over to abstraction with little difficulty. Most outstanding painters of the last fifty years have followed this pattern, a gradual synthesis and development of their work based on a study of the objective world.

The pencil study and the photograph at the right show the Thames River view overlooking the barges in Chelsea, London, a spot made famous in Joyce Cary's novel *The Horse's Mouth* by his character, the artist Gulley Jimson. The painter Derek Middleton lived for several years on such a barge and grew to know the dawns and dusks of many romantic Thames evenings. From these experiences came the small gouache on the opposite page—a study in abstract terms of form and color which has been filtered through the artist's selective process until the painting itself, shorn of all extraneous detail, is there for us to enjoy. The accents of red and green, the subtle suggestions of atmosphere, the fogs and sunset hues have all been synthesized into a new form, an Abstract Impressionism, a new reality.

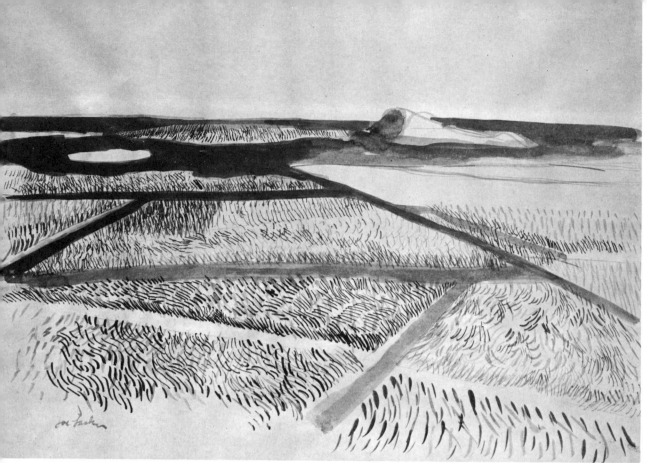

An ink drawing on wrapping paper by Joe Lasker. Repetitions of marshland grasses set against the long diagonal and horizontal lines of infinite space. Simplicity itself, seen and drawn with a selective and sensitive eye.

Amazon River sketch by James Pinto. One of a series of wash drawings using jungle-edge forms in compositions lending themselves to later abstraction.

A wash drawing by Louis Ribak. Exciting forms of rock, wave and sea enliven the page with sparkling calligraphy.

Rapid drawing of crowds and buildings made in Rome. The pipe cleaner technique was used here.

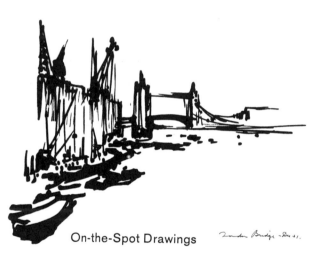

On-the-Spot Drawings

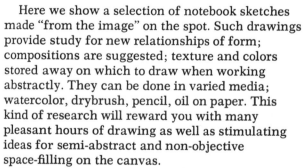

Here we show a selection of notebook sketches made "from the image" on the spot. Such drawings provide study for new relationships of form; compositions are suggested; texture and colors stored away on which to draw when working abstractly. They can be done in varied media; watercolor, drybrush, pencil, oil on paper. This kind of research will reward you with many pleasant hours of drawing as well as stimulating ideas for semi-abstract and non-objective space-filling on the canvas.

There are many arguments for and against working from nature, especially with too much fidelity. Most mature artists combine the two approaches or work in cycles, returning to nature for refreshment after prolonged bouts of studio work and invention. Many, especially the Constructivist and geometric painters, find no need for reference to natural forms; their world comes from deep within, serves their purpose, and is sufficient even within its very limited means and its rejection of imitative forms.

SIENE · /61

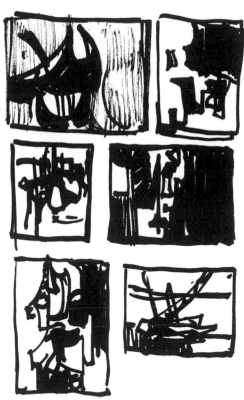

For Muldoaels

Moonflowers
/59

NEW MATERIALS AND TECHNICAL INNOVATIONS

Some of the technical innovations that have come into being to accompany the many waves of contemporary art should be of interest to us at this point. Some of the techniques are new, developed out of the search for new and broader methods of working; many take advantage of the new pigments and binders that have been invented for industrial uses and adopted by the artist. Other techniques exploit new devices that will enable the artist to obtain more textures, more brilliance of color. The use of what might once have been considered unorthodox material—the collage is a good example—has become quite accepted in most galleries in the world and it is not strange to come upon pictures constructed of metal, concrete slabs and thick colored plaster in many advanced exhibitions.

Theoretically, there is no reason why the contemporary artist *should* go on painting in the manner of the van Eycks who invented oil painting. The chances are, from a strictly utilitarian point of view, that a picture painted on a support made from woven glass fiber, prepared with an unchangeable white plastic ground and completed with the finest of acrylic resin paints, will be more permanent than an Old Master's painting which has to be remounted on new linen frequently and whose original oil pigment will inevitably deteriorate. After all, even our houses are now vinyl and acrylic resin coated for longevity and practicality, as are our cars and furniture of the "plastic age."

The preference for a traditional medium has, of course, its advantages. The light canvas support on a stretcher, the "juicy" quality of the standard oil pigment in its vast range of colors already prepared for the painter, the habit of using this medium rather than experimenting with the newer techniques offered by the chemist—these are some of the qualities that have kept oil painting as the major medium used by artists even today.

New Tools

If you have not tried unorthodox tools for drawing and painting, you will find it worthwhile to do some experimenting before you try a major work with them. Changing over to such unusual media can often provide an exciting stimulus for the hand grown somewhat monotonous from habit, or break a facility that has taken on an over-trained manner of working. Some painters have been known to switch to their left hand at times to try their skill afresh. Changing over to an unfamiliar medium from time to time is often a good way to reawaken a tired inspiration.

Drawing with pipe-cleaners may seem odd but I discovered this one day while sketching in Italy. I had lost the felt from the felt sketching pen and needed some device for the same kind of texture-making, to put in tones on an outline drawing in ink. The fuzzy, soft covered wire instruments happened to be in my sketching bag. With them, I found I could make broad passages of broken line, even lines, or spottings that I needed to finish my drawing. Since then I have added pipe-cleaners to my sketching tools. The illustration on page 131 shows a large drawing done completely with them, using black india ink. Use the pipe-cleaners to make dry-brush effects by rubbing out the ink on paper first; bend a tip to shape for broad tonal areas; use the tip as a pen-nib.

Bamboo sticks, cut into shape as pens, match-sticks, feathers and quills, the end of the paint-brush, worn-out and splayed bristle and sable brushes, all of these can be put to good use and will give you qualities and variations from the traditional pointed-brush fashion.

Razor blades for scraping passages through wet ink and watercolor, sponges and paint-rags for daubing on textures or wiping away and dragging paint surfaces are standard, but the use of plastic and hard rubber rollers is not so common. Try laying in a canvas with the large rollers generally used for painting walls. Broad areas can be covered rapidly and with many textural devices. Many artists use flat spatulas of all sizes, some with handles, some merely broad strips of various width of pliable aluminum or steel. Putty knives or broad scrapers of all kinds are employed. Soulages uses a wooden rake-like affair on a stick and works with this on the floor, painting his strong planes of paint as though working in a garden. Pollock's dripping and throwing of paint over canvases is an old and worn story already, but variations of this spattering and dribble technique can still be of value in making certain passages alive and vibrant. Wax crayons, candle wax, chalks and tinted inks—all of these, used as underpaintings and combined with overpaintings and scumblings, can make wonderful visual surfaces. Repellents such as candle wax reject water-paint or thin casein and then color comes alive in a bed of broken textures. Ink over casein, allowed to dry and then scrubbed away under a tap, will make splendid surfaces for the painter to work over with final details. Try many of these combinations, but use *them,* don't let them use *you!*

Pigments and Paints

Science has recently provided many new pigments, malleable and permanent, which were not at the disposal of the artist even a few years ago. Though these pigments and colors do not replace the older media, they do add newer and quicker ways of obtaining certain qualities. Such names as Acrylic, Vinyl Copolymer film and others are becoming as well-known as standard oil paints; many of them are being packaged for the artist and are obtainable at art stores in convenient tubes and bottles. A few years ago, these were only being used by artists who called upon the industrial paint manufacturer for help in order to obtain comparatively minute quantities directly from the wholesale factory. Cellulose-based paints such as Duco have gradually been superseded by the plastic polymer paints in many industries and it is to these that the artists' materials manufacturer has given his attention. A thick permanent paste of fine pigments bound in a plastic binder which is soluble in water, yet dries to a hard, non-porous surface, non-yellowing and permanently flexible, is packaged by several firms under such names as New Masters Artists' Colors, Aqua-Tec, Politec, Hyplar, Liquitex, and others. The absence of a linseed oil binder, which is used in oil painting, permits quicker drying, and an important point—layers can be painted over each other at any time in any thickness without danger of eventual cracking. The advantages of rolling canvas or paper are also evident. Glazes of thin transparent washes over thick impastos may be made and marble dust, and sand imbedded into the adhesive binder of prepared acrylic mediums or gessos.

In spite of the advantages of the new pigments, the oil media has other qualities that its faithful practitioners value and that merit its continued use for some paintings. Its buttery feel has not yet been replaced by the polymers; its slower drying is sometimes an advantage and, to the traditionalist, there is nothing to replace the good smell of turpentine and linseed oil in the sketchbox and studio.

Many artists use a media known as "Lucite." This is added to oil colors as they come from the tube and give the paint flexibility and brilliance. Others use a polymer tempera technique, mixing their own colors with a basic plastic media which comes to them in a milky form but dries transparently. This is a more involved technique and needs much experiment before the amount of pigment, powder and water plus binder may be used for the most easily workable qualities.

For the student, the ready-mixed acrylic paints are the best. If he wishes to use the plastic binders for large and heavily-textured paintings, there are many forms available through industrial sources, but even though more expensive, it is better to use the more refined materials especially prepared for the artist.

As a precaution, all paintings done with plastic materials should be marked as such, warning curators and collectors not to re-varnish with oil varnishes or remove the acrylic film with oil varnish remover or solvents.

Some artists use building cements and plastics, coloring these or spraying them after they have been set into desired textures. Such techniques may be dangerous and it is advisable to use a spray mask and to take precautions by wearing rubber gloves when using some of these plastic cements and binders. Celite, sand, pebbles and other textures are often imbedded into paintings made with a plastic base.

Casein is a popular media, similar to gouache, for making abstract paintings. An opaque, permanent pigment, it has immense possibilities for color and texture making. The advantage of being an emulsion color gives it flexibility; it can be used diluted in water or thickly with textures, though it must not be applied with the heavy impasto of oil paint or used with a palette-knife technique. Careful underpainting with thick white and glazing color thinly over the impasto texture allows fine modulation and drawing when needed. It is ideal for sketching and working quickly as it dries in short order and can be packed away without the nuisance of drying time. A full coverage of its many techniques can be found in a volume devoted to it alone.
(See Bibliography.)

Subject

1 Picture Plane and Pictorial Space

Investigate traditional perspective problems. Depth and recession by other means; Cézanne theory, Cubist's multiple seeing. The fractured image and formalist use of picture plane. Planes and volumes, tensions and thrusts.

2 Basic Abstract Design

Elementary pictorial dynamics. Format. Principles of design used with line, mass, chiaroscuro in contemporary mode. Study of design factors in contemporary painting, sculpture, architecture. Use of natural form as basis for semi-abstraction. Non-objective and Constructivist concepts. Doodles and development into full paintings.

3 Textural Adventures

An important phase of abstract painting. Learn the many varieties of textures possible with traditional and new media. Experiments with new tools on various surfaces and prepared grounds. Paper cuts and collage an essential study medium here. Drawings and paintings from nature.

4 Color Research

Hours can be devoted to the pleasures of color mixing. Explore color possibilities in many media. Combine color in other listed study subjects. Try limited schemes, two and three color harmonies, full palette. Make a close study of Impressionist, Fauve, Formalist and Abstract Expressionist schools noting use of techniques. Read the many fine books on scientific color theory.

5 Study of Natural Form

A series of straightforward drawings and paintings from nature —shells, flowers, rocks, feathers, skies and trees. A number of days devoted to close observation of natural forms. This study will bring endless dividends no matter what manner your final work may take.

6 Some Modern Techniques

Experiments to be made with the many new media awaiting the contemporary artist. Acrylic paints have their own qualities, needing experimentation. Use the new tools, spatulas, etc., Collage and the many types of print-making; at times venture into sculptural forms, and assemblages.

An organized study plan can often be of value to the student with a restricted time schedule. The one here is offered as an aid to time-saving and for progressive work when studying on one's own. This chart is set up similarly to ones I suggested in former books.

in Abstract Picture-making Projects

1 Analytical compositions based on still life groups.
Negative and positive space; depth and recession.
Drawings and paintings from nature developed semi-abstractly.
The pure and formal Constructivist Abstraction.
Study of planes and edges.
Influence of color in recession.
The large canvas fully developed from sketches.   **8 sessions — 4 hours each**

2 The keynote is "do and dare."
Imaginative designs in black and white. Three or more tones in black and grays.
Compositional studies of non-objective kind. Compose in circle and pyramid.
Use abstract alphabet on pages 97 and 98 to construct painting in the
various manners shown.
Investigation of Bauhaus teachings.   **10 sessions — 4 hours each**

3 The simple cut paper design using textured papers and materials.
Study of formal and free collage, marble dusts, etc.
Mixed media, wax repellents, under-paintings, glazings, scumblings.
Use of spatulas, sponges and knife technique for impastos.
Study from nature for texture making.   **8 sessions — 4 hours each**

4 Over the year try a series of paintings; monochromatic (one color in all ranges
of light and dark), a yellow, red, blue, green and other one-dominant hue.
Complementary schemes.
Paintings from nature, non-objective and free gesture experiments
using full palette.   **8 sessions — 4 hours each**

5 Try the close-up view, microscopic if you wish, of grasses, butterfly wings,
a drop of water. Infinite worlds of design await you.
Still-life, landscape and figure.
Use varied media. Paint with large brushes, use a quill pen, charcoal,
work in black and white and color. File away and keep such studies for
later reference when you need inspiration.   **8 sessions — 4 hours each**

6 Panels 12″ x 16″ and smaller for experiment using polymer acrylics.
Work on canvas, masonite, gesso grounds.
Combined brush and palette knife.
Monotypes, paper prints, cardboard edge drawing.
Watercolor and casein techniques for abstract design making.   **1 to 10 hours**

It is based on doing 4 hours of intensive and self-directed study a week. With this number of hours regularly and faithfully covered, 200 hours will be amassed per year—a full 4-week course of 7 hours daily at an art school. This, if doubled in time, would equal a full two-months art school program.

STUDIO / 61

A SUMMING UP

By now it will be obvious that there is no *one* way to think or work as an abstract artist. The ways and means are as diverse and many mannered as humanity itself, the impulses and directions as variegated as the infinite personalities of civilized men. The range of Abstract Expressionism, for example, though at times seemingly caught in one mould, is endless and we can dismiss without concern the portentous words of critics who are always telling us that "Abstraction is finished" or the "Figurative" is doomed. Abstraction in its finest sense has always been with us, hidden beneath the masterpieces of the ages and much of what we think of today as abstract is in reality a "new figuration" which we are learning to understand.

Somewhere in the over-all picture you will find *your* preference, both for certain kinds of painters' works as well as the kind of painting you will want to do for yourself. Don't worry about being derivative or influenced into ways of working. It is impossible not to be, especially at first, and all painters of any worth expose themselves to the efforts of others constantly, for critical values as well as in a competitive sense to see if they can do as well or better. The choice of a manner of working *is* a difficult one but with plenty of work

you will be able to select an approach that is of paramount interest to you. Your ideas and convictions will change as you progress, and from trial and error will come opportunities to forge works with some stamp of your own personal style and direction.

It is a mistake to consciously try for this "trade-mark" of your own too soon, or to find shortcuts, obvious mannerisms or "gimmicks" that will call attention to your work. These can be detected at once by sensitive onlookers and only weaken your statement. An honest effort to paint what you know and understand and a vital progressive attitude toward learning and searching deeper is the only basis for fine work. It has always been thus. For every didactic statement you read or hear you will find an equally contradictory one sooner or later, and you must learn to judge for yourself, weighing closely the many viewpoints of others. Along the opposing roads of countless scarred battlefields of art, you will find some paths that will parallel yours as well as others that seem to go in opposite directions. It is wise to wander down these unknown roads occasionally for who knows what new and fresh visions may lie over the hill or around the next turning?

Keep an open mind and if you have trouble in

understanding abstract expression in painting, begin by freeing yourself from the prejudice that a painting must always represent or imitate *something*. Remember the delights of earlier years when, as a child, you first reacted to the bright colors of the flowers, the glint of silver tinsel, or searched for smooth and magic pebbles, wet and shiny at the water's edge.

Something of this delight is waiting for you in paintings, if you can learn to accept from another sensitive and gifted human being, trained and experienced in expressing the truths of his inner feelings in terms of paint with line, color, shape and form. Perhaps the artist will give you this experience by using *representational* forms, but in the world of painting today it is not *necessary* that he do so. There are many other ways in which he may put down for us his own world of vision and often these reach far beyond the depicting of outward fact or imitation of natural forms.

No matter the style, or what forms the painter may choose in expressing himself, there are basic foundations common to all means and techniques. Some of these foundations have been discussed in this book—structure, unity of conception and consistency of vision. These three precepts could well be engraved on the sketchbox or easel of every amateur and student painter. Figurative or non-figurative, black and white or color, oil or watercolor—whatever the technique, these precepts will serve as a self-critical reminder of what to look for and preserve at each working session.

Their presence, or the lack of them, will reveal the professional touch or amateur concept more quickly than any other element of technique or skillful painting. They are the basic understandings that bring about the over-all impact of the composition, the feeling for the onlooker that everything is in its right place, that nothing could be added or taken away; there is a completeness to the painting or drawing that is unmistakable.

Structure considers the plane surface and the scaffolding of the composition in pictorial space.

Unity implies an organic growth of color, form and technical needs to express a harmonious and complete vision.

Consistency of seeing, either in the mind's eye or in natural forms, is a clear cut and direct manner of expression that does not become confused in a welter of isms, mixed-up styles, and mannerisms.

Armed with these three critical ideas, the student will find that he can correct many things that disturb his pictures, for nine times out of ten he will find that it is not in the little touches or details of the picture that the fault lies, but in this larger and all-embracing concept.

Avoid following the latest mode or fashion but at the same time do not let prejudice of the new keep you from going ahead. In the apparent chaos of values which may seem to engulf you, in the many abuses of the freedoms of painting today, there still exists a steady stream of vital and creative picture-making. Avoid the cheap, transitory and ephemeral, but make sure that your judgment is sound before you are ready to dismiss work that may bother you because it is new or untraditional. There are immutable laws in existence still, though they may be obscured and buried in the rush of our busy lives today, which can help us to sense what is good or bad, both in life and in art. To come near them, to feel within ourselves their wisdoms and needed guidance, is not easy. To know them, we must, like the Chinese philosopher-artists of old, say a prayer and learn how to be humble before the brush touches paper. We must become, in the real sense of the word, artists.

GLOSSARY

Abstract Art. An equivocal term in spite of many "authoritative" definitions. *See* Introduction, page 12.

Abstract Expressionism, Abstract Impressionism, Action Painting. Abstract painting in the styles of the twentieth century using the "free gesture."

Alla Prima. Painted in one go or sitting.

Architectonic. Synonym for monumental.

Art Nouveau. A movement in the nineties using architectural decoration of a curvilinear type.

Assemblage. An assembly of objects and non-art forms to create a sculptural or fine-art expression. "Found" art.

Automatism. A form of free drawing and a type of undirected expression similar to "doodle." A surrealist technique using subconscious impetus.

Bauhaus. A school of fine arts and crafts founded by Walter Gropius in 1919. Klee, Feininger, Kandinsky taught there.

Blaue Reiter, Der. (The Blue Rider) German painters, 1912. Klee, Kandinsky, Marc, Macke, and Muter. The painting style is a combination of Fauve Expressionism and Geometric Cubism.

Broken color. An admixture of several touches of paint causing vibration of color. Color which is not flatly painted in one hue.

Casein. An emulsified pigment with lactic base.

Chiaroscuro. The ordering of light and shadow in a picture.

Classical Abstraction. Formalized abstraction as against pictures by action painters. Disciplined, ordered, and geometrical. Constructivist.

Collage. Papier Collé and collage are almost similar. Often rags, pebbles, and various such oddments are added.

Complementary colors. The primaries, red, blue, and yellow, form complementary colors when mixed in pairs, i.e. red and blue make violet, blue and yellow make green, yellow and red make orange.

Constructivism. Constructions in abstract style for architecture, 1920. Today, a painters' movement renewed in Paris. Descended from Suprematism of Malevitch, 1913. Geometrical forms without representation.

Cubism. Semi-formal transposition of subject through geometrical and "cubed" structure of planes developed from Cézanne's theory by Picasso and Braque, 1908.

Dadaism. Beginning of surrealism during World War I—a protest against tradition, with far-out shock tactics such as the "fur-lined" tea cup.

Decorative. The picture surface ornamented.

Design. Composition planned within the picture plane. Conception of a work of art.

De Stijl (The Style). Originally the name of a magazine in Holland. A movement in which Mondrian and Neo-Plasticism influenced contemporary architecture through Gropius and others.

Divisionism. Use of "broken color." Unmixed pure hues side by side. An Impressionistic technique.

Dynamic Symmetry. See Golden Section.

Emulsion. A vehicle consisting of water and oil. Also casein, egg and some of the modern plastics.

Expressionism. Paintings from the subjective world rather than objective interpretation . . . van Gogh, Roualt, Soutine, and others. Expressive style by exaggeration of plastic means. Emotional painting.

Fauves (Wild Beasts). French painters Matisse, Derain, Dufy, and others, exhibiting at Salon d'Autonne, 1905.

Form. Any volume or plane in the picture.

Formalism. Formal presentation of a subject. Constructivist technique.

Futurism. An Italian movement, 1909, attempting to interpret the dynamic and mechanical modern world.

Gesso overleaf. Plaster of Paris prepared with glue-water for grounds, to paint on.

Glaze. A transparent film of color over underpainting, or used to modify colors.

Golden Section. Golden mean, *Section d'Or.* A form of Dynamic Symmetry known since Euclid. Divides areas into harmonic proportions. The line divides so that the smaller part is to the larger as the larger is to the whole. CB: AC = AC: AB.

Gouache. Colors similar to tempera—generally gum arabic and pigment. Opaque watercolors.

Ground. A coating of the foundation material on which a picture is painted. Gesso, oil and, today, vinyl and polymer plastic whites are used.

Half-tone. Tone value between dark and light.

Impasto. Thick paint which stands in relief.

Impressionism. A derivative term from first exhibition (1874) of Monet, Renoir, Pissarro, Cézanne and others who attempted a new naturalism by painting the light on objects and landscape. New-Impressionism and Post-Impressionism followed.

Imprimatura. Primed ground, sometimes tinted or grayed.

Line of movement. The line that creates a path in a composition to lead the eye from object to object, shape to shape.

Local color. The actual color of the object, unchanged by special light or shade.

Medium. The liquid used as a binder of colored pigments. Linseed oil, polymer resin, and so forth.

Mixed method. Oil glazes over tempera underpainting.

Monochrome. A painting done in one color only.

Monotype. A print made from a wet painting or drawing done on a metal sheet or glass.

Neo-Impressionism. The scientific adaption of Impressionism by Seurat and Signac, 1885.

Neo-Plasticism. See De Stijl.

Non-Objective. Nonfigurative. Not based on visual objects.

Objective painting. Predicated on the objectivity of natural objects and phenomena. Naturalism.

Orphism. A movement created by Delaunay, 1911. Cubistic color orchestration renouncing objects or representation.

Papier Collé. Paper pasted to form picture or designs. *See* Collage.

Perspective. A scientific method of showing natural objects on a plane surface as they appear to the eye. Renaissance invention.

Picture plane. The front plane of the picture surface on which recession into space is made.

Plasticity. Fully modelled, reproducing three-dimensionality in pictorial space. Shapes and forms harmoniously composed with movement of planes and volumes weighed and balanced.

Pointillism. Neo-Impressionist technique developed from Impressionist experiments—juxtaposing small dots or strokes of pure color on the canvas according to a severely systematic plan.

Post-Impressionism. Reaction against Impressionists, 1910. Development of more structural and formal concepts of painting.

Primary colors. Red, blue, and yellow. With white, theoretically all colors can be made by various combinations of the three primaries.

Purism. Reaction to Cubism and analytical painting, 1918. Le Corbusier, Ozenfant, and Brancusi were its exponents.

Rayonism. Creation of forms by radiation of colors, 1909.

Realism. Interest for the actual as distinguished from the abstract.

Recession. Objects receding into space on the imaginary picture plane.

Rhythm. Repetition of accent with reference of each part to the whole.

Significant Form. The specifically aesthetic element in a work of art. Clive Bell invented the term and called it ". . . a universal element."

Space. Positive space in a picture: the object. Negative space: the space surrounding and between objects.

Subjective painting. Expressionism, Surrealism. Personal expression inspired from within.

Support. The wood, canvas, Masonite, or other material on which the painting is created.

Suprematism. Malavich, 1913. A system of pure geometrical abstraction leading to Constructivism.

Surrealism. André Breton, founder, 1924, defined Surrealism as ". . . the chance association of subject matter in dream worlds." Dali, Tanguy and Ernst are well-known surrealists.

Synthetic Cubism. The latter stage in Cubism, more austere and formalized, 1918-23.

Tao. The way. In Chinese painting, the close relationship of daily living and the act of painting, "The heart and hand in accord."

Tachisme. Action painting. The "Blot" technique. Accidental patterns.

Tempera. Powdered pigment with whole eggs, yolks, or whites of eggs used as a binder.

Tension. The gravitational stress between planes in composition.

Texture. Representation of smooth or rough surfaces of objects. The quality of the paint medium itself.

Trompe l'oeil. To "fool the eye." Painting that creates the illusion of reality. A fly, a drop of water on a petal . . . almost anything can be done in this technique.

Underpainting. The preliminary lay-in of design and tonal value; often a thick and neutral impasto over which transparent color is laid; sometimes a thin transparent wash.

Vanishing point. The point on the horizon line in perspective to which all parallel lines appear to recede.

Vitalism. The energized image. The nonfigurative Vitalist expression "charged with life." *See Art into Life*, Wilson, Bibliography.

Vorticism. Wyndham Lewis, 1914. The spirit of the Machine Age expressed in painting. Similar to Futurism.

Zen. Chinese Buddhism. The Zen ideal, "A quiet, self-confident and trustful existence of one's own—to experience life at each moment"; a philosophy important to Chinese painters.

BIBLIOGRAPHY

ABSTRACT PAINTING, Michel Seuphor, Harry N. Abrams Inc., New York.

ART AND SPACE, Aaron Berkman, Social Science Research Council, New York.

ART AS UNDERSTANDING, Frank Avray Wilson, Routledge, London.

ART INTO LIFE, Frank Avray Wilson, Centaur Press, London.

THE ARTISTS HANDBOOK OF MATERIALS AND TECHNIQUES, Ralph Mayer, The Viking Press, New York.

ARTISTS ON ART, Robert Goldwater and Marco Treves, Pantheon Books, New York.

THE ART OF ASSEMBLAGE, William C. Seitz, The Museum of Modern Art, New York.

THE ART OF COLOR, Johannes Itten, Reinhold Publishing Corporation, New York.

ART SINCE 1945, Will Grohmann, Editor, Thames and Hudson, London.

ASPECTS OF MODERN ART: SELECTIVE EYE III, George and Rosamond Bernier, Editors, Reynal and Company, New York.

THE BANQUET YEARS, Roger Shattuck, Anchor Books, Doubleday & Co., Inc., Garden City, New York.

CATALOGUE OF COLOUR REPRODUCTIONS OF PAINTINGS, 1860 TO 1961, Unesco, Paris.

CEZANNE DRAWINGS, Alfred Neumeyer, A Bittner Art Book, Thomas Yoseloff Inc., New York.

CEZANNE'S COMPOSITION, Erle Loran, University of California Press, Berkeley.

THE CHANGING FORMS OF ART, Patrick Heron, Farrar, Straus and Co., New York.

COLLAGE, Janis, Harriet and Rudi Blesh, Chilton Book Division, Philadelphia, Pa.

A CONCISE HISTORY OF MODERN PAINTING, Herbert Read, Thames and Hudson, London.

COURSE IN CASEIN PAINTING, Leonard Brooks, Reinhold Publishing Corporation, New York.

CUBISM AND TWENTIETH-CENTURY ART, Robert Rosenblum, Harry N. Abrams, Inc., New York.

DESIGN AND FORM: THE BASIC COURSE AT THE BAUHAUS, Johannes Itten, Reinhold Publishing Corporation, New York.

DICTIONARY OF ABSTRACT PAINTING, Michel Seuphor, Tudor Publishing Co., New York.

DICTIONARY OF ART AND ARTISTS, Peter and Linda Murray, Penguin Books Inc., Baltimore, Md.

DICTIONARY OF MODERN PAINTING, Fernand Hazan, Tudor Publishing Co., New York.

ENJOYING MODERN ART, Sarah Newmeyer, Reinhold Publishing Corporation, New York.

FOUR STEPS TOWARD MODERN ART, Lionello Venturi, Columbia University Press, New York and London.

GEOMETRIC ABSTRACTIONS IN AMERICA, John Gordon, Frederick A. Praeger, New York.

GISLEBERTUS, SCULPTOR OF AUTUN, Denis Grivot, and George Zarnecki, Orion Press, New York.

HANS HOFMANN, William C. Seitz, The Museum of Modern Art, New York.

IS YOUR CONTEMPORARY PAINTING MORE TEMPORARY THAN YOU THINK?, A Chicago Chapter Artists' Equity Publication, International Book Co., Chicago.

LANDSCAPES, Paul Cézanne, edited by John Rewald, Tudor Publishing Co., New York.

LOOKING AT MODERN PAINTING, Leonard Friedman, W. W. Norton & Co., Inc., New-York.

MODERN FRENCH PAINTING, Sam Hunter, Dell Pocketbooks, New York.

THE MODERNS, Gaston Diehl, Crown Publishers Inc., New York.

NATURE IN ABSTRACTION, John I. H. Baur, Whitney Museum of American Art, New York.

PAINTING AND REALITY, Etienne Gilson, Pantheon Books, New York.

PATHS OF ABSTRACT ART, Edward B. Henning, Cleveland Museum of Art, Cleveland, Ohio.

PEDAGOGICAL SKETCHBOOKS OF PAUL KLEE, Introduction and Translation by Sibyl Moholy-Nagy, Frederick A. Praeger, New York.

THE POCKET DICTIONARY OF ART TERMS, Mervyn Levy, Editor, New York Graphic Society, Greenwich, Conn.

POST-IMPRESSIONISM, John Rewald, Museum of Modern Art, New York.

PSYCHOLOGY OF PERCEPTION, M. D. Vernon, Penguin Books, Inc., Baltimore, Md.

THE SCHOOL OF PARIS, Bernard Dorival, Thames and Hudson, London.

THE VISUAL EXPERIENCE, Bates Lowry, Harry N. Abrams, Inc., New York.

WATERCOLOR—A CHALLENGE, Leonard Brooks, Reinhold Publishing Corporation, New York.

INDEX